A NEW DAWN

Wolfgang Pietrek

A NEW DAWN
Wolfgang Pietrek

ISBN 9781914615597

A CIP catalogue record for this book
is available from the British Library.

Published 2023 Tricorn Books
131 High Street, Portsmouth, PO1 2HW

Printed & bound in the UK

A NEW DAWN

To my wife, Elaine,
and our sons,
Nicholas and Christopher,
and grandsons Julius, Floyd and Lucan

Contents

Introduction

After reflecting for some time on a title for this book. It was with some reluctance that I finally decided on A NEW DAWN. As I drove through France, heading for the channel port of Calais, I was still battling with a feeling of guilt and betrayal. My previous employer who had given me the exciting opportunity to work and study in different parts of the world had obviously considered me for a future position in the company's management team with secure and rewarding career prospects. And then, there is Freiburg, which I now called my home town, which had given me and my family such a warm welcome after our escape from East Germany. It is an attraction to tourists from all over the world and yet I had failed to persuade that maiden from Scotland to make this pearl of the Black Forest our future home. Had I really done the right thing to let my heart overrule my head? Whilst passing through a small village and with all these thoughts whizzing through my head, I had a near miss with a parked motorcar by the roadside. This incidence caused a strange change in my earlier nostalgic deliberations. Yes, I said to myself, there was a lot I had left behind, but a challenging future was waiting for me on the other side of that narrow stretch of water. After all, it was no longer *A Journey into the Unknown*. I was familiar with the language, in my pocket I had an employment contract with one of the country's most reputable companies and, to crown it all, it would enable us after a five-year courtship to take our marriage vows. So, by the time I had reached the outskirts of Calais, the earlier flash of guilt and nostalgia had been completely replaced by the invigorating feeling and conviction that I was truly ready to welcome this dawn of a new day.

A Choppy Crossing

A strong northerly wind churned up the sea but, showing complete defiance to this, the powerful ferry continued her passage to Dover. And not before long, a faint silhouette of the white cliffs appeared on the horizon. It almost felt like a homecoming and yet the finality of my break with my continental past left me also with feelings of unease. Will it remain a journey into the unknown? My recent travels had certainly led me to believe that I could easily immerse myself in the Anglo-Saxon culture and way of life but then at that time I was only a visitor. Will I ever reach the stage where deep down I will not feel a foreigner on this island?

Well, Joseph, you might as well make yourself comfortable again. I will shake up the kaleidoscopic tube once more and hopefully it will let us participate in the joys and challenges of a plethora of events which are about to become my new future.

Surely, Wolfgang, with your love life now seemingly heading for a safe haven, an employment contract with a company of international repute in your pocket, you must be feeling on top of the world.

Thank you for those encouraging words, Joseph. You are absolutely right but it has always been in my nature to weigh up potential setbacks before crossing a road. This underlying feeling of caution may well go back to the days in my teenage years when, in unfamiliar surroundings, I had to avoid capture by East German or Russian border guards when making my trips across the Iron Curtain. Although I could by now claim that Britain was not an unknown territory to me any more, would I in due course become a true islander? I remembered that only earlier this year the newspapers in Freiburg were full of articles about the French government strongly opposing Britain joining the European Economic Community because they described that country as a vassal state of the USA and unsuitable to be part of the European post-war family. I remember that at the time, many voices in Germany assigned these French views to the realm of historic Anglo-Gallic rivalry, but was that stretch of water, albeit very narrow, after all a divide that turned them into European outsiders?

As an enthusiastic member of the European Youth Movement in the 1950s, the concept of reconciliation and collaboration with all Western European nations had become a Leitmotif for my own political orientation. It certainly would have given me extra comfort and assurance to know that my new host country can at least be part of this European Family of Nations.

The new modern system of roll-on and roll-off ferries allowed a rapid disembarkation and possibly thanks to the new spark plugs I had had inserted before my departure from Freiburg, my little DKW's engine started at my first attempt. I followed the vehicles ahead of me to the Dover Border and Customs Control, noticing already the signpost warning motorists to drive on the left side of the road. It suddenly struck me that this would be the first time that I was actually driving on the left myself rather than being the passenger as had happened in the past in Scotland and Australia.

In spite of the large number of vehicles, my passage through the controls was quick and uncomplicated. The Border Control official just gave a cursory glance at my work permit and after yet another stamp in my passport I was quickly waved on to make room for the next car behind me.

According to my roadmap, my target − Harrogate − was 500 kilometres further north and would be a full day's journey. Once again, lucky circumstances came to my rescue. Prior to my departure from Freiburg, my parents had received a letter from my long-lost cousin Edeltraud, informing them that she was now married to an English gentleman and that she lived in a small town called Reigate, not far from London. Luckily she had also added her telephone number to her full postal address. Shortly after I had left the port area, I noticed one of those familiar red telephone booths on the roadside. I thought to myself, why not give her a surprise call and maybe I can even stay there for a night before proceeding north to Harrogate. Then I could also meet her English husband. After another quick glance at my road map, I gathered that it would not take more than two hours from Dover.

A rather official-sounding voice answered my call. "Bob Butcher here, who is calling?" When I identified myself, his voice changed very quickly and I heard him shouting out for Christine to come to the telephone. And there she was, my cousin Edeltraud, now known under the less Germanic name of Christine.

Our last encounter was in the late 1940s in Rostock in East Germany and since then we had lost contact with each other. Her voice trembled with excitement when I told her that I was in Dover and that I could be in Reigate within the next two hours. I have to admit, I was equally excited about this reunion and the opportunity to share our life experiences during all those past years. Yes, of course I could stay as long as I wanted to which she added that since Reigate is a rather sprawling conurbation, I should telephone again when I reach the outskirts and Bob would come to guide me back to their home in Raglan Road. I felt really elated to have made this telephone call and to know that I could start my first day in my new home country with a member of my own wider family.

As I drove out of Dover, I suddenly noticed that my petrol gauge had almost reached its lowest point. With focusing my attention predominantly on how to get to the ferry harbour in Calais, I had completely forgotten to look at my petrol gauge. With a wad of French francs still in my wallet, I could easily have filled up the tank again on my approach to Calais. But too late now.

The road out of Dover was rather steep and with the petrol tank nearly empty I was getting worried that it might not make it up that steep road. Thankfully the sign for a petrol station appeared on my left halfway up and with a sigh of relief I pulled in. A middle-aged pump attendant looked decidedly puzzled as he walked round my car, muttering something to himself. He finally turned to me saying, "I have not seen one of these before. How many gallons do you want?" With that, he was about to unscrew the cap of the petrol tank to insert the nozzle of the pump hose when I told him to stop as I had to first convert the gallons into litres to establish how much oil I needed to put into the tank before filling it with the correct amount of petrol. I had made it a habit of always carrying a can of oil in the boot of my DKW and inserting the oil into the tank myself before letting pump attendants fill the tank with petrol. The poor man here in Dover was utterly bewildered by all this and it was obvious that cars with two stroke engines were a rarity in the UK. Nevertheless, after we had completed the whole procedure and I had paid my first petrol bill in England, the attendant wished me a good onward journey.

With my steering wheel now on the wrong side, my progress to Reigate was rather slower than I had expected as I was very reluctant to attempt any overtaking of other vehicles.

It was over two hours before I finally reached the outskirts of Reigate and, as suggested by my cousin, I stopped at a telephone booth again to let her know my location and to seek the suggested assistance to guide me to their residence in Raglan Road. Her husband Bob arrived within a very short time and, following him through a maze of roads, I began to wonder if I could have managed it all on my own.

The house in Raglan Road was a very impressive residence as were most of the buildings in that road. Their ground-floor apartment was spacious and I could see that my staying overnight would not inconvenience them in any way. In her letter to my parents, my cousin had only mentioned that she was now married but had not divulged that she was also the mother of two little boys.

The whole evening turned into a memorable feast, not just in a culinary way but also with indulging in shared memories about our childhood days, her holidays with our family in Rostock, the visits to the glorious beaches at Warnemünde and boat rides on the River Warnow. Then of course I had to recount my own foreign travels during the last few years and disclose the reason for my own sudden return to England. There was certainly enough material to make it a memorable and interesting evening. I now also learnt that after the war my cousin had decided to seek a new life in Canada where she met her husband Bob, a tall gentleman of English descent. He however had not intended to make Canada his new home and a year after their marriage they resettled back in England.

Bearing in mind that you and your family had such a challenging and eventful escape from East Germany, did you learn more about how your cousin reached the West in those turbulent post-war years?

Strangely enough, Joseph, in spite of raising this topic several times, my cousin avoided giving me any clear answers and reverted back to stories about our childhood days and how she now liked living in England. It was only many years later that I learnt the true reason for her reluctance to speak about her traumas during that tumultuous post-war period.

The following morning, having been provided with a bag full of fruit and provisions, husband Bob marked my road map with a suggested route to Harrogate, which to my horror meant driving right through the centre of London. Having avoided driving through Paris only a few days ago because of the density of traffic, the thought of now driving through an even busier place like London, filled me with considerable apprehension. However, Bob assured me that drivers in this country are more considerate and forgiving than their continental counterparts and that once the early morning traffic had subsided I should have a reasonably easy passage through the metropolis. My mind flashed back to my first arrival in London in 1957 and the friendly taxi driver who seemed so at ease behind his wheel whilst providing me with a memorable sightseeing tour of his city.

Heading North

And so, with promises of keeping in touch I set off north for London and the Great North Road. And Bob was right. Even with my steering wheel now on the left and wrong side of the car I began to feel increasingly confident in crossing junctions and it seemed as if other car drivers were actually making allowances for my occasional hesitancy. Or maybe they were intrigued by this strange-looking foreign car. After crossing the River Thames near the Houses of Parliament I also began to recognise road signs for landmarks and districts of the city which I had visited or heard about during my training period in 1958 at the Coats Warehouse on the Great West Road.

I felt very pleased with myself when I reached the northern outskirts of the city and when I saw a sign for Welwyn Garden City I knew that I was finally on the right road to the north of the country. In fact, looking at my road map, this arterial highway continued all the way up to Edinburgh in Scotland.

Considering that my DKW had only a small engine which in the past had already shown signs of overheating when travelling non-stop for long distances, I was very pleased to see her performing so well on this journey. Maybe driving on the left side of the road was more to her liking.

At the next stop for petrol, the pump attendant was again intrigued by this foreign-looking car and when I asked him to stop filling the petrol tank until I had finished putting oil into the same tank he simply had to tell me that they do not make cars like that in his country. I think he added that these types of engine are mainly used for lawn mowers.

With my supply of oil now running very low, I asked the attendant to add a can of engine oil to my bill.

Soon after leaving the petrol station, I noticed a road sign with a very familiar name on it. It was Leicester, which triggered off fond memories of my training spell there in 1958 and the wonderful hospitality I had received from Mr Chapman and his wife. Once I have settled in Harrogate, I thought to myself, I must re-establish contact with that amazing couple who at the time had contributed so much to make me feel welcome on this island.

It was a very rural landscape with fields stretching right to the horizon but only a short while later the scenery became interspersed with signs of industrial activity. Pit heads, winding towers and large slag heaps were an unmistakable sign that I was now approaching an important mining area. And not before long I passed a road sign, showing the way to a town called Doncaster. Soon the scenery changed again to a completely rural environment and after having passed another road sign with the name Leeds on it, I knew that my final destination was only a short distance away.

As per my road map marked by Bob, I left the Great North Road at a village called Wetherby and with daylight already beginning to fade I finally pulled up outside the Granby Hotel in Harrogate, feeling elated and exhausted at the same time. It was the 25th of June 1963. As I had hoped for, my telephone call to Elderslie was received with great jubilation by both mother and daughter, who, I suspected would probably have celebrated this event that evening with a great feeling of satisfaction for having successfully masterminded my exodus from my own homeland.

With my work only starting on 1st of July, I had ample time to familiarise myself with my new home town and above all to find suitable lodgings. The letting agency specially recommended a large and inexpensive room in a property very close to the Granby Hotel in Slingsby Walk, with views over the wide expanse of the Harrogate Stray. I liked the sound of it and as it turned out it became my home for over one year. My landlady was an elderly widow who shared the house with her large Airedale dog but was clearly very keen to also have some human company. Later on, as time passed by I was almost treated like at son and it was not long before even the Airedale dog began to greet me in a boisterous manner when I returned from the office in the evening.

My landlady seemed to have no family of her own but a niece and her husband came to visit her at frequent intervals. It soon became very obvious that the relationship between the niece and her husband was strained, with the niece inflaming the situation even more by openly trying to flirt with me. It must have been during such a visit just before Christmas, when, after having retired to my room, the young lady rushed into my room with a flushed face and clearly in a state of utter distress, throwing her arms round me and begging me to run away with her. Having no experience in dealing with such emotional onslaughts I was absolutely dumbfounded and after disentangling myself from her embrace I eventually persuaded her to go downstairs again to her husband and to have a calm and adult discussion with him about their future. On reflection, Joseph, it all had the hallmark of a scene from one of those Hollywood films, depicting the emotion-driven and unpredictable actions of a desperate and unhappy wife. However, my response to her grotesque and also embarrassing proposition must have been the right advice, because the next morning a more relaxed couple set off on their journey back to their home in Colchester. This dramatic episode however did not sour

our relationship in the years to come and the unfortunate event at Slingsby Walk was never mentioned again. The following year, on one of their return visits, the husband, a gifted artist, presented me with a large oil painting with the calming scene of a small country brook which has been adorning our home to this very day.

Early in the morning of 1st July 1963, I drove to Hookstone Road and after passing the gatehouse to the office site, I parked my car right in front of the main office building. I had only just walked through the entrance door when the receptionist told me to remove my car and to move it to the designated car park. "Those places out there," she said with a rather stern voice, "are only for directors and senior staff." That was a good start, a reprimand before I had even started my new job.

After a brief introductory tour of the office building, I was asked to fill in some forms with personal details and most importantly also my newly opened bank account into which my salary could be paid. Within the company structure and grading scheme I was now a TO (Technical Officer) with the grand salary of £1,041 per year and a member of the company's comprehensive health insurance policy.

With all that done, I was officially introduced to my new manager, the very same person who had interviewed me only a few months before. "I am glad it has all worked out well in the end," he said. "I am pleased to have you in our team."

The whole atmosphere in the building was very different from that of the Coats Headquarters in Glasgow. None of the male employees streaming in through the front entrance wore a bowler hat and the average age seemed to be much lower. My office was spacious but sparsely furnished and

I was to share it with another young man called Fred. Before lunchtime, the manager had already convened a departmental meeting at which he announced my future role. I was to promote and monitor the company's business in certain West European countries with special emphasis on the key markets of Germany and France, where ICI's polyester patent rights were due to expire in the near future, thus bringing to an end the royalty income from the continental licence holders. The prospect of future business trips back to the Continent was music to my ears.

With an interesting and seemingly also secure future ahead of me, all was now set to start discussing plans for our wedding. Our future residence in Harrogate was accepted as a bearable compromise as it was only a four-hour car journey back to Elderslie. But with the question of housing still to be resolved, we all agreed that a formal announcement of our wedding should not be rushed. Then there was also the question of money for the required down payment for our future home.

It must have been early November when I was asked to visit the ICI offices in Frankfurt to meet the members of the newly created department for the Fibres Division. This provided me with a wonderful opportunity to pay a brief visit to Freiburg, not only to bring my parents up to date with my new life in England but also to cancel my account with the Wuestenrot Building Society and to withdraw all my savings.

My parents showed admirable understanding when I explained to them that once again I would not be sharing Christmas with them. In any case, I said, we shall soon have a date for the wedding which will bring the whole family together.

A week-long trip to the company's agents in Greece

and Cyprus concluded my travels for the rest of the year. The Christmas and New Year break in Scotland turned once again into a flurry of visits to the wider family and friends. This time, however, I was not only showered with congratulations on having become a resident in the UK and questions about my new employment but also with the well-meant remarks that surely the wedding must now be within sight, to which I could only reply that Elaine's mother was probably the best person to ask.

Intensive socialising, I concluded, can be very stimulating but if stretched over several days can also lead to mental and even physical exhaustion. I felt quite happy when on a frosty morning I and my DKW set off again on our long journey south.

Back in Harrogate, I became more and more immersed in my new job. I especially appreciated the spontaneous inclusion into the social circles of several of my colleagues. One of them, John Petrie, especially went out of his way to let me share many happy hours in the midst of his family which led to an enduring friendship.

It was a dark and frosty evening in early February when, arriving back at my lodgings, my landlady was already standing in the doorway with a piece of paper in her hand. "This came by special delivery this afternoon," she said. As I looked closer, I saw it was a telegram. I have always had an instinctive fear of telegrams because people only seemed to send them when they got themselves into a difficult situation and were then pleading for immediate help or the news was of a tragic nature. It was a telegram from my brother Dietmar with the devastating words:

Papa gestern gestorben. Bitte komme schnell. (Papa died yesterday. Please come quickly.)

Since my landlady's house did not have a telephone, I

immediately rushed off to the nearby Granby Hotel. My attempts to learn more about our father's sudden death were only met with my mother pleading with a quivering voice to come as quickly as possible. Surely, it must have been an accident, I thought to myself, because during my brief visit to Freiburg, only as recent as last November, my father had looked fit and well. It was a grim start for 1964 and certainly cast a cloud over any plans for an early wedding. I had so much wanted both my parents to be present at our nuptials and also to gain a personal experience of my new host country.

When I saw the manager the following morning to ask for special leave, he immediately instructed the company's travel office to book an open-ended ticket for the next available flight to Basel. "You will have numerous and onerous tasks ahead of you," he added, "and your mother will appreciate your company now more than ever, so take your time." It all reminded me of the paternal attitude which I had treasured so much with my previous employer. I began to think that this might be a general hallmark of management in large British companies.

After a brief telephone call to Elaine's mother to give her the sad news, I was informed that an early afternoon flight would be available and that a company car would take me to Yeadon Airport. After a quick detour to Slingsby Walk to collect my passport and a few personal belongings, we reached the airport just in time to catch the London-bound plane for the first leg of my onward journey to Basel.

It was late in the evening when I finally reached our home. My mother looked rather ashen-faced but she had clearly regained her composure and was able to provide me with a more detailed account of what had actually happened.

As had been his habit for several years, my father had returned to our home for his lunch break when my mother decided to quickly make a few purchases at the nearby grocer's shop. On her return, she found our father stretched out on the floor, halfway under the table in our sitting room. "At first, I thought, he had fainted," my mother said, "and I quickly phoned our house doctor to ask for his advice. He suggested to feel my father's pulse whilst he was waiting on the telephone." To her horror, my mother did not feel any pulse at all and she also noticed that his hand was going cold. Our doctor then told my mother that he would immediately summon an ambulance to take my father to the hospital. When the ambulance arrived, the medical member of the crew carried out various checks on my father's body after which he turned to my mother and said, "I am very sad to tell you that your husband has passed away. We shall do a fuller investigation at the hospital to establish the cause of his death." It was already the following day that our doctor phoned back to inform my mother that my father had suffered from a cerebral haemorrhage caused by a large blood clot. And he was only 55 years old.

The following days were very stressful for all of us. Thankfully my father had always kept a detailed account of all his commitments, insurance policies and banking details which made it so much easier for us to unwind all his affairs. The one thing missing was any form of a written will but as there was no family fortune to distribute, that did not really matter.

The tragic events in the immediate post-war years and the prolonged separation in our family following my father's escape to the West, had almost by necessity led to a stronger bonding with my mother. And yet, when I looked at him in the chapel of rest, memories came flooding back of his care and warmth, especially during my pre-war childhood days, our summer outings to the beach at Warnemünde, trips into the forest to gather berries and mushrooms and sitting with him on the shores of the River Warnow telling me to watch that little float in the water in case a fish had taken the bait. And then those wonderful long train journeys to our paternal grandparents in Upper Silesia. All this created a sudden deeper closeness. And here I was standing now to say my final goodbye.

I do not know, Joseph, if you yourself have been in this position before, but it is a very strange and scary feeling when, at the end of all the proceedings and all the well-meant condolences from friends, colleagues and acquaintances, one finally returns to one's home, knowing that one chair round the dinner table will from now on remain empty.

Considering the tragic circumstances and the unexpectedness of my father's death, my mother maintained her composure remarkably well. In a way I felt sorry for my brother Dietmar who, at his young age, was now left on his own to fill the gap for all the missing male members of the family.

I had really expected that my mother would plead with me to prolong my stay in Freiburg but she almost urged me not to overstay and to return to my new place of work. "Let us hope," she said, "that your new responsibilities will bring you back to Germany more often and that it might give you an opportunity to visit us from time to time. It would have been nice to have had you here for your birthday next Sunday but no doubt, Elaine will also treasure your presence very much."

Our parting at the Freiburg railway station became rather emotional. It was one of those rare occasions when my mother could not hold back her tears and I was not far from doing the same. Whilst waiting for the train to arrive, I suggested to my mother that with the death of our father, 1964 might not be the correct year for our wedding. "Your father and I have been watching for many years now if and how this relationship will ever be resolved," she said, "and I am sure he would hate to be the cause of any further delay." I could not have asked for better words of comfort and encouragement.

It was the 11th of February when, after a swift transfer in London, I reached Yeadon Airport again.

It must have been a day or two later when the export director called me to his office. Had I done something wrong during my recent visit to our agents in Greece and Cyprus? It was my first face-to-face encounter with this gentleman and when he started to ask me about my own personal and professional background it quickly became clear that I had not been summoned to his office for any form of reprimand. He was quite a jovial sort of person and clearly a devoted pipe smoker. Whilst I was reporting my background to him, I remember him lighting his pipe twice and, on both occasions, after blowing out the match and without turning his head, he threw the match over his shoulder and it landed precisely in the wastepaper basket behind him. I wondered how many days or weeks he must have practised to achieve this level of precision.

I assume you were not merely called to his office to give an account of your own background and to witness his skills in throwing matches into a wastepaper basket?

No, after giving me a short summary of his own military career and his involvement in liberating Rotterdam from the occupying German forces, he told me that he was looking for a person to organise the six-monthly meetings of the European Spinners Club consisting of key customers in the

UK and several continental countries. The next meeting was due very shortly in Zurich, he added, and he wanted us to be in charge of the proceedings. Considering that I was still a relatively new recruit to the company, I felt very pleased with being offered this opportunity. "My secretary will give you the file on our Club," to which he added that "I will meet some very important people for our business."

This meeting turned out to be the beginning of an action-filled and interesting working relationship in the years to come.

Meanwhile, the most pressing issue was a weekend visit to Scotland not only to report on the tragic events in Freiburg but also to seek further clarification on a likely date for the wedding. I also needed to let Elaine and her mother know that whilst the observance of a certain period of mourning over my father's death would be expected, my own mother had suggested that this should not lead to a further delay beyond the current year.

It became obvious very early that both Elaine and especially her mother were determined to turn our wedding into a glamorous event with almost military-style attention to detail and planning. Drawing on her good knowledge of UK fiscal regulations, Elaine's mother suggested that September would be the most appropriate month as it would secure tax relief for newly married couples for two fiscal years. This certainly was not going to be a case of simply taking the train to Gretna Green and sealing our bond over the anvil at the famous blacksmith shop.

Knowing now that after a four-and-a-half-year period of seemingly insurmountable problems, September 1964 would put a final seal on this drama I was filled with a great sense of relief. I also knew that Elaine's mother would leave no stone unturned to make it a festive and memorable event.

When Elaine mentioned that she would try to get a transfer from her present job at ICI in Scotland to the company's Fibres Division in Harrogate, I realised the time had come for me to seriously think about looking for a home for us in Harrogate or somewhere nearby. Elaine was only too keen to come to Harrogate to start the house hunting within the next month.

Remembering my mother's plea to write more regularly, I gave her a full account of my visit to Scotland and the high probability of a September wedding.

The memory of my father's death was gradually overtaken by a flurry of preparatory activities for the wedding and my growing portfolio of responsibilities in my new job.

It was quite a relief when I was summoned by the export director again one day to be told that the time had come for another meeting of the European Spinners Club and that our Swiss Club member had now confirmed to host the meeting in his country. The suggested venue for the meeting would be the Baur au Lac Hotel in Zurich.

With that, I was given a sheet of paper containing the director's handwritten points for the agenda. "From here on," he said in his laconic manner, "it is up to you now to get this show off the ground." With the Club consisting of only five members, the preparatory work was quickly concluded and on a dull April day the director and I set off for Zurich. I felt very privileged to come face to face with these people from the UK, Denmark, Austria and Switzerland who were clearly seen as important trendsetters in the use of ICI's polyester fibre.

The atmosphere at the meeting resembled that of a jovial family gathering. All the Club members knew each other very well and I was warmly welcomed as the future

Club Secretary. The whole trip was an interesting and also enjoyable experience and was the forerunner to many more joint overseas visits in the years to come.

Back in the UK, Elaine's mother had not wasted any time in firming up the arrangements for a September wedding. The date was to be 23rd September, with the marriage to take place at the Baptist Coats Memorial Church in Paisley which she and Elaine had recently joined as worshippers. It felt quite strange that after my guilt-filled departure from my previous employer, my marriage to Elaine should now be sealed in a church bearing their name.

At long last, I now had a firm date which set in train an action-filled programme of preparing for an event which had eluded us for so many years. In fact, there had been quite a few moments when I thought that it might never take place.

How many members of my family and my old circle of friends should I invite? Would they be willing to travel all that distance to Scotland? Are my savings I had withdrawn from the building society in Freiburg enough for a down payment on a small house here in Harrogate or in one of the nearby villages? Having looked at the windows of local estate agents, I soon realised that my own financial resources were only enough to cover a small portion of any purchase price, even for a modest dwelling. With our family always having lived in rented accommodation, the ramifications of house ownership and methods of financing a purchase were unfamiliar to me but I was very fortunate in being able to obtain sound advice from Elaine's mother. She assured me that with Elaine and myself being employed by one of Britain's most notable enterprises we should not have any problem in securing the necessary finances for our first home.

On one of their joint visits to Harrogate, our house-hunting efforts led us to the picturesque nearby village of Knaresborough where, on a new housing development by the Wimpy Company, we found a house which not only seemed affordable – albeit with the help of a sizeable mortgage – but which also met with the approval of both mother and daughter. I felt quite chuffed at the idea of soon becoming an actual house owner. On top of all this, Elaine mentioned that there was a possibility of obtaining a transfer from the company's Scottish Nobel Division to the Fibres Division in Harrogate. It all felt like finding the last few pieces in a large jigsaw puzzle.

All this news was enthusiastically received back in Freiburg, with brother Dietmar even asking if he could bring three of his own school friends to witness a Scottish wedding.

On one of my return visits to Elderslie, Elaine and I were invited by the Minister of the Coats Memorial Church for a pre-marital counselling session. He was a charming gentleman who in a fatherly fashion reminded us of the need of utter commitment to each other and the importance of tolerance in the years ahead. He was indeed very complimentary when he realised that our relationship had already survived nearly five years, founded on no more than correspondence and rather infrequent personal encounters.

The following weeks flew by at unbelievable speed and crammed with tasks I previously thought never existed. The house purchase in Knaresborough was completed, the husband of Elaine's longstanding school friend Mary agreed to be my best man and with Harrogate being my place of residence arrangement was put in place for our wedding bans to be read out at the little church just a few hundred metres away from my lodgings in Harrogate.

Up in Scotland, Elaine's mother seemed to have a firm grip on all the necessary arrangements. Her cousin David Balfour was to 'give away' Elaine, and his daughter Clair was going to be the bride's wedding trail bearer. The bridesmaids Sylvia, Yvonne and Edith had been chosen from Elaine's circle of friends and family and all the necessary arrangement for the accommodations of my own family members and friends were firmly in place. Also my cousin Edeltraud from Reigate had not been forgotten. The groom, I was told would spend the last night before the wedding in the nearby house of Mr and Mrs MacFarlane, the parents of Betty, who thanks to Elaine's letter I was fortunate to have met during my stay in Hong Kong. To crown it all, I now learnt that the wedding reception would be held in our favourite seaside place, Largs, at a place called Curling Hall.

Even the arrangement for our honeymoon was quickly resolved, with a start-off in a hotel at one of Scotland's celebrated locations, Loch Lomond, and then an escape to warmer climates in Spain, Morocco and Gibraltar.

Was there anything else for me to do now but to turn up, properly attired and celebrate the moment when finally Elaine and I could put a final seal on all those years of seemingly insurmountable problems?

The Grand Finale

And then it really did all happen. With families and friends gathered in this beautiful church, a magnificent memorial to my previous employer's devout commitment to the Paisley community, Elaine and I finally exchanged our vows of marriage in front of the big marble baptismal fond. It was only later that I learnt that Elaine's wedding dress was the same one her mother had worn at her own wedding to Elaine's late father. Cousin David performed his role as Elaine's escort in a very accomplished manner, in fact so well that in the years to come he was asked to lend his arm to four more young ladies on their walk down a church aisle.

It was a sunny but windy day and quite a crowd had gathered at the foot of the church. The word must have got around that the groom came from Germany. When we reached the bottom of the huge number of stone steps I heard a young boy shouting to a group of contemporaries, "He is the owner of Volkswagen!" I decided not to disillusion him, but it clearly demonstrated that Elaine's mother's organisation of the whole event had almost created the public impression of a major society wedding. She certainly did not do things by half. Even the canine members of the family, which by now had risen to two, had to have their participation recorded in the final photo of the newly-weds. It did not really come as a surprise to me because a few months earlier Elaine had already stated to me that from the outset there will be three in our marriage with the instant family addition being her pet dog Mitzi. Compared with all the other obstacles of the past, this was one of the easier demands to accept.

Curling Hall in Largs turned out to be a magnificent venue for our reception and once again Elaine's mother had shown her organisational talents by ensuring that this part of her daughter's big day was also staged in a lavish style. Whilst not being able to match the eloquence of my best man Alex I managed at least to perform the opening dance with Elaine in a more accomplished fashion compared with my rather clumsy performance when we first met at Makerston House.

At the end of this most joyful and high-spirited event I really felt that I had become part, not only of this new family, but also their friends and acquaintances. And from all I could see, I was sure that this new bond was also welcomed and treasured by our mothers. Our departure was crowned by me being hoisted into a large baby cot and carried shoulder high outside the hall where Elaine was already waiting in our getaway car.

As the new day dawned and I looked over the wide expanse of Loch Lomond from our hotel window, I could once again feel the magnetic power of the surrounding countryside, something which I first experienced during those memorable days when touring the Highlands as a trainee salesman. And on top of all this, a beautiful young maiden of this intriguing country had now become my wife. What a journey it had been.

Having become so accustomed to journeying on my own in the past, our honeymoon added a new dimension to the world of travelling. No longer a case of throwing a few essential items and a change of clothing into a small suitcase plus a quick TPM (Ticket-Passport-Money) check. No, now it became a major planning operation to cover all the possible sartorial needs for our multi-location journey to the Mediterranean region. For our chosen destinations,

Torremolinos, Tangier and Gibraltar, the travel agent had thankfully assured us that even at this late part of the year we could still expect pleasantly warm temperatures which helped to at least keep our luggage at only two, nevertheless large, suitcases.

Torremolinos turned out to be a charming and welcoming seaside resort with a colourful high street and a few hotels, some with direct access to the magnificent beach, stretching out for several kilometres. The whole place exuded all the characteristics of a typical Spanish coastal settlement and we both felt that it was a wonderful starting point for our honeymoon. The occasional visit by a donkey to our beach hut only added to the unspoilt and almost romantic atmosphere of this place. As you will probably know, Joseph, within a span of only a few years Torremolinos, together with so many of the picturesque settlements along the coast, became the target of an ever-increasing wave of tourism. Along with so many other villages on this magnificent coastline it lost a great deal of its charm and originality. As I learnt later, Torremolinos in particular rapidly turned into a popular and commercially vibrant holiday hub for the sun-hungry tourists from northern Europe.

Well, on this occasion you seem to have got your timing right and you two can at least look back with happy memories on this idyllic and crowd-free setting.

Yes, it would not have needed much persuasion to spend the rest of our honeymoon in this place but then the deep-seated human urge to explore new places had already led us to making it into a multi-destination journey.

Our next stop, Gibraltar, quickly catapulted us back into Little England with Royal Mail letterboxes, the reassuring sight of the traditional helmeted English Bobby and a myriad of shops with familiar names in the main street.

All this provided an instant feeling of comfort and security aided by the presence of that famous Rock, towering like a giant protector over the whole city. Having by now become quite accustomed to left-sided road traffic I was quite surprised to see that this outpost of the Empire had been allowed to follow the continental way of driving on the right. The restaurants and open-air coffee shops in the Casemate Square provided a relaxed blend of Englishness and Mediterranean laissez-faire.

Whilst Gibraltar was only our transit point on our way to Tangier, our two days were completely filled with not only exploring this fascinating city but visiting the imposing caves of the Rock and being amused by the antiques and acrobatics of the resident monkeys.

The majority of our fellow travellers on the ferry were Moroccan men who I presumed had found employment in Gibraltar and were returning to their families for the weekend. Soon after our departure from the Gibraltar harbour, with the Rock still dominating the backward view, the silhouette of the African coastline appeared in front of us. A well-dressed fellow traveller standing next to us at the ship's railing volunteered the information that on a clear day the African coastline could also be seen from the Rock.

It did not take long before the coast ahead of us revealed more of its mysterious settlement. Rooftops seemed to stretch out on a gentle slope from the coastline into the hinterland. A tall tower-like building dominated the centre of this panorama and the early morning sun provided a warm glow to this fascinating picture. It had all the makings for an exciting part of our honeymoon.

After a noisy disembarkation and finally emerging at the exit of the long reception hall with its large ceiling fans, young boys and middle-aged men descended upon us like an avalanche, offering to carry our suitcases, pointing us to waiting taxis or carrying posters with names of hotels. To our great relief we finally spotted a man holding up a sign with the name of our travel agent. He welcomed us in fluent English and after a short drive on what appeared to be a coastal road, he finally delivered us to our hotel on the eastern outskirts of Tangier.

The interior of the hotel left you in no doubt that you now were in an Arabic country. In the entrance hall you were greeted by a pleasant aromatic smell and a receptionist in a colourful outfit. The view from the comfortable room led directly to the nearby beach, an expanse of golden sand as far as the eye could see. Our travel agent had done really well in selecting this place for our triple-location honeymoon. The thought of now having a few days to explore an alluring and mysterious place like Tangier became more appealing by the minute. The sight of a group of camels passing sedately along the edge of the beach added to the sensation that we had crossed into a different world. Elaine was particularly struck by this as all her past travels had been to the touristic regions of continental Europe.

A large array of leaflets in the hotel foyer sent out a clear message that this was not just a place for sun-seeking beachcombers but an ancient and exotic town with a multitude of attractions for foreign visitors. Even day-long excursions into the rugged mountains of the Berber tribes.

Outside the hotel, taxi drivers were noisily offering their services. Their deafening clamour was yet another new experience as it contrasted so vividly with the restrained behaviour of taxi drivers in most European countries. Amongst all this noise we suddenly heard a voice in clear English. A well-groomed young man with a clean-looking car offered us his services. In fact he turned out to be such a friendly and knowledgeable person that we decided to use his services for the whole duration of our stay.

The lure of this intriguing city was such that we spent very little time on the nearby beach.

It must have been on our second day, when the driver took us right to the Grand Arch leading into the Medina. We had just left the car and arranged the timing for our return journey to our hotel when a cheerful looking young boy approached us with the offer to be our guide and helping us to find the best bargains in this labyrinth of shops and stalls. He introduced himself as Mustapha and was probably not more than 12 or 13 years old. His broken English was good enough to maintain adequate communications between us. We felt tempted to ask him why he was loitering around during daytime when he ought to have been at school but when we looked around and saw other youngsters of a similar age, manning street stalls or walking in the nearby alleyways carrying baskets and buckets with a variety of fruits and local produce, it struck me that the rather rigid educational norms of nearby Europe may not necessarily apply here,

After passing through the impressive archway, we found ourselves engulfed in a different and exotic world. Alleyways in all directions and wafts of strange smells filled our nostrils. The plethora of goods on display was overwhelming and the gesturing by most of the stall holders, begging us to enter their premises added to a sense of utter confusion but also amazement. To people like us, used to doing our shopping in orderly rows of high street shops and fashion houses, this vibrant hub of commercial enterprise provided a wonderful new experience, particularly for Elaine who until now had not travelled outside Europe.

Whenever we stopped to look at trays with unusual Berber

jewellery or intricately woven prayer mats and rugs, or in fact at any of the many things on offer, our young volunteer guide quickly assured us that he knew much better places where to get bargain purchases. And so, after meandering through a few more crowded alleyways we finally ended up at a rather modest-looking stall where Mustapha's appearance was greeted with much noise by two bearded middle-aged men. "Meet my uncle," Mustapha joyfully exclaimed, pointing at one of the two men. "He will make you good prices but first we shall have tea."

The modest-looking shop entrance certainly betrayed what lay behind it. Beautiful carpets of all sizes, a seemingly endless array of hand-crafted copperware, pieces of furniture with ornate fittings and inlaid designs, cabinets with traditional jewellery and local artefacts and a long row of traditional garments.

Surely, you must have gathered by now that your young urchin guide was hanging out at the entrance to the Medina to make sure that his eventual clients would spend their pounds or dollars at premises owned by his family or other reward-promising establishments?

You are absolutely right, Joseph.

Having come across this form of promotional posturing before on my previous foreign travels, I suspected from the outset that this was also Mustapha's role when loitering outside the Medina gate but then I also had to admit that this was all part of a touristic experience. On top of all this, Mustapha was a really likeable little chap and Elaine had also taken to him.

The tea drinking turned into a rather ceremonial affair with small, sweet cakes being passed around. Mustapha's two bearded relatives could converse in English quite fluently and seemed interested in hearing more about our own background and our reason for visiting Tangier. More surprisingly, they abstained completely from encouraging us to purchase anything from their enormous range of merchandise. The wondering eyes of Elaine became particularly fixed upon a row of leather pouffes, which she thought would make an attractive and also practical addition to our new home in Knaresborough. By emptying the pouffe of its present inner stuffing it would also easily fit into one of our suitcases. Very practical thinking, I thought.

After concluding our purchase without the traditionally expected process of haggling, Mustapha suggested that we follow him to see another shop in the Medina but we insisted that he took us back to the entrance gate for our prearranged taxi ride back to the hotel. It struck me that there were probably several more members of Mustapha's wider family who had stalls in this buzzing commercial labyrinth and who also counted on Mustapha's skill to bring potential clients to them.

Back at the main entrance, our taxi was already waiting for us. We thanked Mustapha for his services with a generous gratuity but when he offered to be also available the next day, we declined as we were quite keen to do some of the exploring on our own.

The following day we decided on an early start. Having read some of the promotional leaflets in the hotel foyer we felt that a visit to the Kasbah would be a worthwhile target for the day. It sounded like a real historic gem of this intriguing city. The taxi driver suggested to start off the day with a visit to the Central Café, a popular meeting place for locals and foreigners. We agreed also to make this our pick-up place for the afternoon.

Listening to the conversations at neighbouring tables and seeing the titles of newspapers read by several middle-aged gentlemen it left one in no doubt that this settlement on the most northern tip of the African continent was also very much a place with a legacy of several European cultures. The Kasbah, we had learnt, was the old Medina of Tangiers, and with its narrow, shadow-providing lanes and alleyways gave visitors a true feeling of antiquity. As we ambled down the Rue d'Angleterre we passed a church which, despite its Moorish architecture and a bell tower resembling very much the minaret of a mosque, turned out to be an Anglican Church named after the Scottish patron saint St Andrew. A lasting symbol of Britain's involvement in the various periods of foreign administrations through which this strategic settlement had passed over many centuries.

When we entered the magnificent entrance hall to the Kasbah Museum, we could hardly believe what we saw. There, sitting on a marble bench and with a big grin all over his face was Mustapha. We had deliberately not disclosed any of our sightseeing plans when we parted company with him the day before and here he was right in front of us. When I asked him if this was yet another location where he offered his services as a tourist guide he replied that he had been waiting specially for us. Obviously the gratuity we had given him the day before had marked us out as a lucrative target with expectations of more to come. I tried to find out from him how he had known that we would be visiting this place today but he refused to divulge his secret and instead merely implored us with pleading eyes to allow him to be our guide for the duration of our stay in Tangier. With only two more days left, one of which we had in any case decided to spend in leisure on the beach in front of our hotel and having been truly impressed by his extraordinary skill to trace us, we agreed to his request. With that issue settled, Mustapha promptly took on his lead role again, describing with considerable eloquence the origins of some of the exhibits and the importance of the halls we were passing through, mentioning repeatedly that this was after all the original palace of the Sultan of Tangier.

On our way back to the city centre we passed the Anglican Church again and Mustapha did not miss the opportunity to show off his knowledge of local history. "This church," he explained, "was built during the reign of your Queen Victoria, a lasting sign of your country's connection with our city. In honour of our own local culture," he added, "the centre nave of this church points directly towards Mecca and inside the church is a full version of the Lord's prayer engraved in Arabic."

Unfortunately, the gate to the church was closed on that day. The names on the gravestones in the adjacent cemetery were visible evidence of the number of Europeans who had chosen this location as their final resting place.

After a leisurely walk back to the Central Café and some refreshments with Mustapha, we agreed on the timing for the next day, thanking him again with a gratuity for his services. It did not escape my notice that even in this place, several bearded clients waved their hands at Mustapha and gave him a friendly smile. Maybe his sudden appearance in the Kasbah was not so mysterious after all.

After another very interesting sightseeing trip with Mustapha through other picturesque parts of this bustling metropolis we finally parted company and, after spending our final day on the sandy beach at the hotel, we finally set off with our friendly taxi driver to board the ferry to Gibraltar. It was the 7th of October and still pleasantly warm.

It was not long before the contours of the famous Rock appeared again in front of us. Our travel plan included one more day in Gibraltar. As the Rock moved nearer by the minute, I suddenly found myself cast back to my teenage years in post-war East Germany when our history teacher missed no opportunity to tell us about the impending collapse of the British Empire and the atrocities during the struggle for independence in India. And yet, here we were about to set foot again on a happy and peaceful little gem of that allegedly crumbling Empire, which to me appeared to be almost a microcosm of the land only a few hundred kilometres further north.

After a short taxi ride to our hotel and check-in we enjoyed the rest of the day just strolling through the streets again with leisurely breaks at cafés and restaurants. The highlight was a random encounter with a middle-aged Swedish couple who engaged in a casual conversation with us. When we told them that we were on our honeymoon and due to fly back to England tomorrow, they asked if we would like to join them for dinner at their hotel that night. "We are staying at the Rock Hotel. Come at 6 pm for some pre-dinner drinks," they suggested. It all sounded too good to be true.

On our wanderings through the town we had already gazed at the majestic setting of this hotel with the Rock as the dominant background. The thought of now actually dining in that place, although a wonderful finish to our honeymoon, filled us with some trepidation. At the end of our holiday our apparel was clearly in need of being freshened up again and would fall well short of the sartorial standards expected at such an upmarket hotel.

When we voiced our concern to this friendly couple, they simply said, "Come as you are." Nevertheless, when we finally returned to our own downtown hotel we changed into our outfits which we had earmarked for our return flight to Leeds the next day. With that done, Elaine felt decidedly more relaxed as she, like probably most members of the female gender, has a general tendency to pay stronger attention to sartorial appearances and correctness than me.

It was a glorious evening and from the terrace we witnessed a majestic sunset over the Straits of Gibraltar. Unfortunately, we lost contact with this friendly and hospitable couple who provided us with such an uplifting end to our honeymoon.

Whilst we were enjoying our carefree time in sunny climates, Elaine's mother was busy organising the transfer of all our wedding gifts and furniture to our new home in Knaresborough. Above all, once back home, Elaine would be able to cuddle her poodle Mitzi again, now a key member of our new household.

As we left the Leeds/Yeadon Airport building I could not help feeling a little anxious about our DKW car. I assumed that October temperatures in Yorkshire had been considerably lower than what we had enjoyed recently and I knew from past experience that this could cause problems starting the car, particularly after such a long spell in an open-air car park.

I put in the ignition key with some trepidation and to my great relief, Suzi – a pet name I had given my DKW – sprang into life immediately.

Back in Knaresborough, Elaine's mother had done a truly magnificent job. After an emotional welcome and a rapturous, tail-wagging reunion between Mitzi and Elaine, we did our first round of inspection of our home. All the furniture purchased at Cochrans of Paisley had safely arrived and had been given the appropriate place in the house. Our DKW however was denied its rightful place in the garage as it was full of big tea chests containing crockery, dinner plates, glasses and a multitude of household items gifted by family members and friends. In fact, it took us weeks to clear out these chests but, in the end, the DKW also got its proper home.

I am sure you both must have felt very happy and proud to be the owners of your own home now considering all the ups and downs of the past.

Very true, Joseph, but to put it bluntly, it was probably a much more uplifting experience for me than for Elaine, who after all had just given up the comforts of her mother's imposing house on a hilltop in Elderslie. My family had never aspired to house ownership, and we always lived in rented accommodation. After our escape from East Germany in 1950 we even had to rely on the generosity of a family in Freiburg to share the limited space of their rented quarters with them. For me, this truly was the beginning of a new chapter.

With Elaine securing a secretarial job with one of the senior executives of the ICI Fibres Division and my own position in the Export Department being enhanced by additional territorial responsibilities, life became quite hectic. We also started to build up a social circle and enjoyed exploring the dales around Harrogate and the large variety of traditional country inns. After all the work Elaine's mother had done for us in setting up our new home, we also felt obliged to visit her up north in Elderslie as often as we could. For Elaine it was clearly always a homecoming but I have to admit that I also appreciated the hospitality shown to me by friends and all the members of the wider family.

One weekend we decided to visit Elaine's close school friend Mary and her husband Alex, who had been my best man at our recent wedding They, like so many Scots and Northerners had been drawn by the lure of the Great City and now lived in London. My DKW performed well down the M1 motorway when suddenly the engine started spluttering. It was just south of the Watford Gap roadside compound when the engine stopped altogether and all attempts to get the car started again failed. It certainly was not due to lack of petrol and a visual check to see if there were any loose or broken wires also gave me no clue as to the reason for Suzi's sudden demise. As we were trying to push the car onto the soft shoulder a van stopped alongside us and the young driver asked if he could be of any help. The sign on the van indicated that he was working for a laundry company. "I am not a mechanic myself," he explained, "but I can give you a lift to the next stop on the motorway where you can telephone for further help. I am on my way to London," he added. When we told him that we ourselves had intended to travel to London to visit friends he immediately offered to take us all the way to the nearest bus or underground station in London. We very much appreciated his offer. We quickly transferred our luggage and our dog Mitzi into his van, locked our defunct car and, with me sharing the driver's cabin seat and Elaine and the dog huddled up amongst the laundry bags in the rear of the van, we proceeded with our journey to London.

In the end we got a taxi on the northern outskirts of London and reached Mary and Alex's apartment in reasonable comfort. After some lengthy search through directories and also helpful advice from the Automobile Association, we eventually managed to find an automobile recovery company who were willing to pick up the stricken vehicle at the Watford Gap. I asked them to bring it back to the garage and car dealership in Harrogate who, having serviced the car before, were hopefully capable of restoring Suzi back to life.

Despite the distressing circumstances on our journey to London, we had a memorable and enjoyable time with our hosts. The train journey back to Leeds and Harrogate was very comfortable but I cannot deny that whilst sitting there in our cosy compartment I could not help thinking about the upcoming cost of retrieving our treasured car. Was it time to say goodbye to her now and invest in a new vehicle thus also getting a steering wheel on the right-hand side? A reliable car was essential for us to get from Knaresborough to the ICI offices in Harrogate and our visits to Scotland.

Back at the office the place was buzzing with excitement. ICI had finally severed its partnership with the Courtaulds Company and was now the sole owner of the prestigious firm known as BNS or British Nylon Spinners. This opened up a host of new marketing opportunities in Europe. On top of all this I was informed that my new job remit would include not only the African continent and China but to my surprise also the countries behind the Iron Curtain. This really surprised me as my personal records, held by my employer and also documented in my West German passport, showed that my place of birth was Rostock, located in the communist German Democratic Republic, the very country we had escaped from in 1950. What would happen when for instance I crossed the infamous Checkpoint in Berlin or visited any of the other communist countries of the Soviet-controlled Eastern Block? Would my name be on the list of wanted persons?

I thought long and hard if I should accept the job remit for the countries behind the Iron Curtain but decided in the end to accept this challenge. And in the years to come it led to memorable encounters and experiences.

When our stricken motorcar arrived back in Harrogate it became clear that any further long journeys would be risky and with the next long trip ahead to Scotland for the Christmas and New Year festivities we decided to say goodbye to Suzi and acquire an 1100 Austin Morris. It was quite an uplifting feeling to drive a new car with the steering wheel on the right side and a four-stroke engine that did not require petrol mixed with oil.

As to be expected, the Christmas break in Scotland was dominated by a series of visits to members of the wider family, including the now almost traditional visit to the MacKellar family in Greenock.

Did this time of the year not make you feel a little homesick?

It did indeed, Joseph, particularly this year when my mother and youngest brother Dietmar were all on their own. I also missed the fairyland atmosphere of the German Christmas market with all its glitter and the waft of roasted sugar almonds lingering in the air. My mother's Christmas tree was always a sight to behold with real candles and lavish hangings of lametta. Yes, I missed all that, Joseph, and consoled myself with the hope that next year Elaine and I could spend the festive season in Freiburg with possibly even some skiing on the nearby Black Forest slopes.

Venturing East

B ack in the office, my newly acquired responsibilities resulted in an ever-increasing volume of travelling, initially mainly to the Mediterranean countries. To learn more about the business world behind the Iron Curtain I started to attend receptions at the London embassies of most of the Soviet Bloc countries. The Bulgarian Embassy on a road right behind Buckingham Palace became one of my favourite places as it seemed to draw a wider variety of attendants than even the Soviet Embassy at Highgate. It was there also that I met a Greek gentleman, Mike Miliangos who in the years to come became a close friend and counsellor. He himself had been forced to flee from his native Greece to West Germany as his political views were regarded reactionary by the then ruling Greek military junta. His wide-ranging business interests led him to travel extensively throughout Europe with London being a frequent destination and during our first meeting he quickly impressed me with his knowledge of doing business with state-controlled organisations behind the Iron Curtain. He drew particular attention to the autumn trade fair in Leipzig which he regarded as the most important place where, in those Cold War days, the East could speak to the West. He indicated that he himself would attend the next autumn fair and that I should join him

The thought of visiting Leipzig was particularly appealing to me as it would provide me with the opportunity to see at long last the St Thomas Church to which, near the end of the war, I had been invited to sing as a guest chorister with the famous Thomaner choir. This choir, founded as far back as 1212, is probably the oldest choral ensemble in the world and at one time counted Johann Sebastian Bach as its choirmaster. Unfortunately, Allied bombing of the railway lines leading into Leipzig stopped me from reaching the town at that time.

I told my new Greek friend that before visiting the Leipzig autumn fair I had already received a request to visit the East German Textile State Trading Organisation in East Berlin. I confessed to Mr Miliangos that with my place of birth Rostock clearly shown in my West German passport I had a feeling of unease about this first return visit into the GDR. Whilst in the end I would have to accept the risk of going, I would find it easier if on this occasion I could travel in the company of the holder of a UK or other West European passport. "I am on excellent terms with senior members of the Ministry of the Interior in the GDR," my Greek friend replied, "and I will come with you to Berlin. Fix your date and fly to Hamburg first where I now live. I will then take you in my car to the Alpha Checkpoint at Helmstedt and from there on straight into Berlin. Once you have finished your business dealings with the East Germans, I will take you through Checkpoint Charlie into West Berlin from where you can fly back to Britain." All this sounded very reassuring and I decided to go ahead with it. Finally, on 7th of June, after a very comfortable run on the Hamburg-Berlin motorway, we reached the border crossing point. It all began to bring back memories of my teenage days, when in the immediate post-war years my initially successful crossings of the Iron Curtain finally ended in the unfortunate capture by Russian and East German Border guards whilst trying to cross the River Werra near the village of Creuzburg, finally ending with a trial by a military tribunal and a few days of imprisonment.

I was already quite nervous when we approached the western side of the checkpoint where the border official merely took a cursory glance at our documents before waving us on to enter the no-man's zone. Just looking at the stern faces of the East German border guards, one got the feeling of unease and coldness. One of the guards pointed us to a parking place outside a barrack building with the entrance flanked by two more uniformed guards. Once inside the building, we faced a long table and a row of other travellers talking to the passport controllers and also to staff in civilian clothing. Whilst waiting in the queue I had noticed already that some passports, having passed their initial examination, were subsequently pushed through a narrow slot in the wall behind the reception table. When it came to our turn, my Greek friend's passport was quickly returned to him with the laconic remark to proceed to the exit and to continue his journey. He insisted however to stay in the building and wait for my passage to be cleared as well. And just as well he did, because my passport also disappeared through that infamous slot in the wall, a sign of some trouble ahead. My Greek friend sprang into action straight away. He spoke to what appeared to be the senior officer and requested access to a telephone to speak directly to a certain high-ranking person in the Ministry of the Interior. The mere mentioning of that person's name in the Berlin Ministry had the astonishing effect of the officer disappearing through a door at the end of the building and a minute later reappearing smilingly with my passport in his hand and wishing us a good journey. With the passport back in my pocket, I had a feeling of new-found freedom and expressed thanks to my Greek friend for his successful intervention. "Knowing the right people," he said, "is even more important here in the East than it is in the West."

The visit to Berlin and the first contact with the state-controlled trading organisation for textiles culminated not only in a sizeable order for ICI's polyester tow but gave me the confidence to rapidly increase my efforts in other Iron Curtain countries. I was now really looking forward to my forthcoming visit to the autumn trade fair in Leipzig.

On top of all this, Mike Miliangos decided to invest some of his own money to build a Crimplene-producing factory in Southern Germany thus not only being a guide and mentor to me on dealing with the East but also becoming a direct customer for our products in West Germany. Clearly being quick in spotting business opportunities, he saw the potential for this new product which opened up new fashion trends for easy-to-care garments. Little did I know at this stage that in the following year I would be organising a fashion show in Prague with glamorous Czechoslovakian models on the catwalk promoting Crimplene dresses and gents' suits.

Our annual leave was spent in Scotland touring the Highlands and visiting some of the locations which I remembered from my earlier days as a trainee salesman of my previous employer Messrs. J. & P. Coats. My longstanding friend, Walter Koch in Munich, had asked if his daughter Barbara could spend the holiday with us to which we readily agreed.

Back in Harrogate my return to the office was somewhat overshadowed by an event which on reflection did not come as a complete surprise. One of my colleagues in the Export Department, a middle-aged gentleman, had lodged an official complaint that my now senior position to him should be withdrawn because he, as a Jewish refugee from Austria, would find it abhorrent to work under a German superior. The whole affair was discretely handled at a very senior level in the company with Mr Harris, the export director, playing a leading part. Strangely enough it was my wife who first informed me about this complaint as she was the secretary to the company directors to whom my Jewish colleague had first voiced his discomfort. In the end the gentleman was given some other responsibilities in the Export Department and we continued to maintain an at least courteous working relationship. The whole episode brought home however that Germany's brutal persecution of the Jews would continue to be a shameful and gruesome heritage which would haunt generations of Germans to come, wherever they are.

With ICI now in full control of marketing the products of British Nylon Spinners, my own job remit had widened considerably. An ex-BNS gentleman, Mr Ash, became our new overall departmental manager and I soon established an amicable accord with him. Nylon yarns, once so vital for producing parachutes and ladies' stockings, had suddenly found an additional new function in the manufacture of what became known as pantyhose. With the arrival of the mini skirt, the pantyhose became the safe protector of female modesty and the business was booming.

After a brief visit to our agents in Greece and Cyprus, the time had come to prepare for my first visit to the Leipzig fair. My Greek friend had promised to attend the fair as well. The BEA flight to Leipzig was smooth and uneventful and on arrival I was quite impressed with the orderly passage through the arrival process. None of the stern-looking border guards we had experienced at our first border crossing at Helmstedt. The only setback was that hotels were all fully booked. However, the lady at the booking desk gave me the address of a private family who could offer me a room at a very reasonable price. My first thought was that this must obviously be a family, checked out by the communist authorities for their firm belief in a Marxist world order and who would not succumb to Western influences. The taxi took me to a street with neat-looking terraced houses and, as it turned out, within walking distance of the fair grounds. The door was opened by an attractive-looking young woman with two little girls standing behind her. "We had expected to host an overseas guest this year," she said, "so please come in and I will show you your room. My husband will be back from work very soon and you can then settle the financial arrangements with him." It was not long before the husband arrived. He looked a little older than myself and of a very jovial disposition, expressing his hope that I would feel comfortable in their home during my stay in Leipzig. Meals, with the exception of breakfast, were not part of the lodging arrangements but the couple asked me to join them on my first day, also for the evening meal. I gladly accepted.

During the meal the conversation was held to a minimum but I could see it in the faces of the two little girls sitting opposite me that they were anxious to learn more about the stranger at their table. To my surprise however, as soon as the meal was finished, the parents asked them to retire to their bedroom. After the two girls had gone, my hosts explained the reason behind their action. "We have done it for their protection," they said, "because in their innocence they might mention something they hear here tonight to their school friends and from there it could be a short road to the ruling authority." Remembering my own schooling days in the GDR I could readily understand their concern.

It soon became obvious that my hosts were very interested in not only hearing more about my own background but also about life generally on the western side of the Iron Curtain. Despite their own critical comments about life under a communist regime, which I found quite astonishing,

I had a feeling of unease. Was it all a trap? Why was I told at the airport that there were no hotel rooms available and then given this private address, whose residents must have gone through a thorough vetting process before being allowed to host foreign visitors? With all this on my mind I remained cautious with my responses to their questions but as time went on I felt more assured that I was regarded as a true fee-paying guest. When I told them that my own mother was born and bred in nearby Zwickau the whole atmosphere became even more relaxed and we kept talking late into the night. In the end I developed a real fondness for this family and I returned to them three more times in the years to come.

With my Greek friend's help, useful contacts were established with several Eastern European State Trading Organisations. A newly emerging feature of selling to some of these organisations was the need to set up barter arrangements to overcome their chronic shortage of Western hard currencies. That meant searching for Western visitors who had come to the fair to make purchases from these very same organisations and then link such purchases with sales by Western suppliers to these very same organisations. This often resulted in lengthy meetings between three parties leading on one occasion to a rather unorthodox outcome. At the fair I happened to make the acquaintance of a gentleman from New York who represented one of the large American fur-trading companies. He was negotiating a large purchase of mink peltry from Romania. In return for a modest commission he offered me the dollar value of his planned purchase for a barter deal, to which the Romanians also agreed. With all that in place I was able to secure a most welcome order for our ICI polyester products. The New York gentleman must have been equally pleased with the deal because when we met up again a year later he surprised me with an unexpected present.

Finally I also managed to visit St Thomas Church, a visit long overdue since 1944, when I had been invited to be a guest chorister with the famous Thomaner Choir. Unfortunately, air raids on the railway line leading to Leipzig had made that visit impossible. Now I had made it. Approaching the church via a lane with attractive houses and ornamental signs over several doorways I was surprised by the height of the white bell tower and its almost baroque-like architecture. The central nave was flanked by five white columns on either side and behind the rather ornate pulpit I saw the stalls of the choristers, one of which I had been invited to occupy in 1944. Being a Lutheran church now, it lacked the feeling of opulence so often displayed in Catholic and Orthodox churches and cathedrals. But then there was the famous organ above the main entrance, played at one time by the great musical director and organist Johann Sebastian Bach himself and in later years also by Richard Wagner. Before leaving the church I quickly sneaked back to the chorister stalls and sitting down in one of them I silently gave thanks for my good fortune.

Back in the UK I returned to a more sedate lifestyle. Elaine, apart from her work at the office, had continued to make our new home even more comfortable. It seemed our dog Mitzi must have missed me more than my wife, judging by the welcome they both gave me. To celebrate my return, we had a delicious dinner at one of the restaurants right on the banks of the River Nidd. It was owned and managed by a Swiss gentleman with whom we became very friendly and whose exquisite cuisine prompted us to many more visits in later years.

In November, a visit to our newly formed Fibres Division

Department in ICI's main offices in Frankfurt gave me the opportunity to also make a brief visit to see my mother and brother Dietmar in Freiburg. After my father's death, my mother had decided to give up the old apartment and to move into some smaller accommodation. Many of the old familiar pieces of furniture had to be abandoned but I noticed that amongst the few pieces that had survived the move was the large clock in a mahogany casing which was originally in our old sitting room. "You may find this very strange," my mother said, as I looked at it comparing it with the time on my own wristwatch. "It stands at 1 pm which is exactly the recorded time on your father's death certificate." Although the clock was fully wound up it must have stopped at that moment and never restarted again.

I invited my mother to spend the forthcoming Christmas and new year with us in Knaresborough or possibly even make a joint visit to Scotland but she suggested to leave it until the next year. She was thrilled to hear about my visit to Leipzig and when I indicated that this may become an annual event, she reminded me that her sister Trudel still lived in Zwickau. After so many years of separation she would be delighted to see a family member again. I explained to my mother that visas for attending the Leipzig Trade Fair excluded visits to other parts of the GDR but that with my past experience of circumventing restrictive rules, I would try my best. "Please do not risk anything," she said, "you have been in enough trouble with that regime before."

The Bamboo Curtain

With the year-end approaching, foreign travels finally came to an end and plans could be made for another festive season in Scotland. The year's closure however was slightly marred by an unexpected occurrence in the office. It came to light that one of the junior clerks, whom I had entrusted to sell waste products from our Wilton Plant to accredited waste merchants in Holland, had in fact arranged significant shipments to one of those Dutch firms. He managed however to understate the weights shipped and had collected monetary rewards from the customer for his fraudulent action. Instant dismissal was unavoidable.

Our festive season in Scotland ran along the same pattern as in previous years with visits to friends and family and warm and generous hospitality extended wherever we went.

On our drive back to Knaresborough I indicated to Elaine already that my export director had warned me of a heavy travel programme for the new year. Not only did he want to see an expansion of our business in the communist countries of Eastern Europe but to also establish contact with the People's Republic of China. When he learnt that in my previous employment I had already concluded business with the People's Republic but with their trade delegates visiting Hong Kong, he suggested that we should meet them on their home ground now and that a visit to the Canton Spring Trade Fair could be the door-opener to that potentially huge market.

It was music to my ears and would mean my third visit to Hong Kong. But this was not going to be a two-to-three-day trip and Elaine's observation that our marriage seemed to be a sequence of sporadic encounters was probably not far from the truth. Thankfully she was enjoying her own work at the Harrogate offices which clearly made my frequent absenteeism more bearable. Our ever-widening circle of friends also helped to ensure that she had interesting and caring company on those occasions, supplemented from time to time by visits from her mother.

The turmoil of the Chinese Cultural Revolution had led to more protracted procedures of obtaining the necessary visa. Attendance at the Canton Fair required first of all an official invitation from the Chinese Trade Authority. That problem was quickly overcome as ICI's office in Hong Kong representing several other members of the ICI Group had already a longstanding history of trade with the Chinese Republic and had an open-ended access to the Canton Fair.

Finally the big day arrived. Elaine and Mitzi drove me to Yeadon Airport as the first stage of my long journey to Hong Kong. Our parting at Yeadon Airport must have had quite an emotional effect upon Elaine because on my return two weeks later she confessed to me that she had completely forgotten how to get back from the airport to our home in Knaresborough and that she ended up in Pateley Bridge where some person finally redirected her back to Harrogate/Knaresborough.

After a 12-hour flight with stopovers in Rome and Singapore, the BOAC 707 finally landed at Kai Tak Airport. Once again I was amazed by the skill of the pilots, just skimming over the rooftops of the buildings on their final descent onto what appeared to be a dangerously short runway. On all my travels, flying into Kai Tak Airport was certainly the most exciting and breathtaking experience.

The passage through the immigration and passport

control channels was swift and courteous and in the entrance hall a man in a smart uniform was holding up a placard with my name. He welcomed me to Hong Kong, took my suitcase and asked me to follow him. I could not believe my eyes. It was a gleaming Rolls Royce. I knew that the company had booked me into the well-known Peninsula Hotel in Kowloon but I had not expected to be collected from the airport in such luxury.

Entering the elegant entrance hall brought back memories of my first visit to this famous hotel. It was during my previous employment with the J. & P. Coats Company that I had a most enjoyable afternoon tea here with Betty MacFarlane, a friend of Elaine's family. At that time, she was the chief matron at the Kowloon Hospital. I promised myself to telephone the hospital once I had reached my room.

Did you not feel tempted to phone also your old colleagues in the J. & P. Coats agency in Jardine House?

It had crossed my mind, Joseph, but you may not believe this, even at this stage I carried a subconscious feeling of guilt in me for having left that company after the almost parental care and the opportunities they had extended to me. In the end I decided not to renew my contact with Jardine House.

My elegant room exceeded my expectation and was the most luxurious accommodation I had ever stayed in during my years of travelling. Unfortunately, I was only booked in for two nights. A small leaflet on a coffee table advertised an in-house tailoring service with made-to-measure suits provided within 24 hours. Never ever having had a tailor-made suit in my life, I could not resist this tempting opportunity and after enquiring about the likely price ranges I told the receptionist that I would be ready for this service within the next hour. And so it happened. A well-dressed Chinese gentleman arrived with a wad of cloth samples from which I could choose something of my liking. "All fabrics are from first-class English weavers," he pointed out, "and lightweight qualities are normally preferred in this part of the world."

After taking my measurements he told me that he would return in four hours for my first fitting and that the suit would be available the next morning when payment would also be due. I was thrilled with the whole arrangement.

When I phoned the local ICI office I was surprised to learn that they had already been informed about my arrival in Hong Kong by our Harrogate office. I was told that I would be joining three other ICI representatives for this visit to Canton. We should all meet the following day at the ticket counter of Kowloon railway station for the 3 pm train to the border station of Lo Wu. Ian, the head of the ICI office, advised me to purchase sufficient personal hygiene products and also my preferred cigarettes, if I were a smoker, because Western goods were not available in Canton. "Do not bring items in sealed tins and I also advise you to leave your camera behind as it will most likely be confiscated." Having heard all this, I was quite relieved when he added that he himself would accompany us four divisional representatives to Canton to make sure we all get settled in well for the fair.

At 9 am the following morning my tailored suit duly arrived, and a quick try-on confirmed it to be an excellent and smart-looking fit. After completing my shopping in nearby Nathan Road and checking out of the Peninsula Hotel, I walked to the Kowloon railway station to meet up with my ICI colleagues, who were representing the interests of three other sectors of ICI's wide range of activities, i.e. pharmaceuticals, dyestuffs for the textile industry and fertilisers. Ian, the administrative head of ICI's Hong Kong office, was to accompany us to Canton and being a Mandarin speaker he promised to look after our welfare during the fair.

In case we got separated during our journey, we were told to remember to head for the Dung Fan Hotel in Canton where he said rooms had been booked for all of us. When I told my colleagues about my own background and my experiences of crossing the Iron Curtain, Ian jokingly remarked that I can now add the Bamboo Curtain to my tally.

When I was resident in Hong Kong during my employment with J. & P. Coats I never had the opportunity to visit the so called New Territory. Now I was going to travel right through Hong Kong's hinterland, passing not only the grounds of the University but also the famous Sha Tin racecourse. I knew from past experience that betting on horses was a widespread hobby amongst the local population. I had witnessed their passion for horseracing myself when I visited the Happy Valley racecourse on Victoria Island. On certain days there were no horses racing at Happy Valley and yet the stands were crowded with spectators watching actual races from Sha Tin on big cinema screens.

It was only one hour before we reached the border station. By this time, very few travellers were left on the train and the majority of them were clearly Europeans, who like us were heading for the Canton Trade Fair.

We left the train with our belongings and were told to take a narrow fenced-in footpath to a building ahead of us which was the Republic of China's border post and as it turned out also the railway station for our onward journey to Canton. I had expected to be received by heavily armed border guards or soldiers of the People's Army but once inside the building we were greeted by friendly-looking and

English-speaking officials who very thoroughly scrutinised our passports. The customs officers were a less welcoming group of people who rummaged quite roughly through our belongings.

Finally the five of us re-joined on the platform of the Chinese railway station where a train was ready for the remaining journey. Again, I had to change preconceived perceptions. I had expected to find the train interior of very basic standard, possibly with wooden seats and no luggage racks, but again, the Chinese sprang a surprise on me. The train interior was in fact of very high quality with soft and comfortable-looking seats, plenty of luggage space and to add to the luxury, the headrest of each seat was covered with a piece of delicately crocheted needlework. I managed to secure myself a window seat and enjoyed every minute of our nearly two-hour journey to Canton.

Outside the Canton station we left it to our Mandarin-speaking leader to organise two taxis, agree on a price and get us to the Dung Fan Hotel. Again, Ian ensured that we were given good-quality rooms with beds covered by mosquito nets, which, as the days went by, I appreciated very much as a practical and necessary help for a good night's sleep. We soon discovered that the whole hotel was only available to visitors from Europe. Visitors from Japan and other Asian countries were confined to a separate hotel, and they were not even allowed to visit any business friends they may have had in our hotel. Each guest at the Dung Fan Hotel had his own nominated room boy. We were never quite sure if these young men were meant to look after our well-being and security or whether their service included also reporting any of our activities back to the authorities. I suspected the latter to be the case.

I had already been warned that negotiating business

with Chinese State Trading Organisations is like a war of attrition. On every visit I made I was received with friendly smiles but also with a range of new questions to which my answers then had to be referred to some technical authority for further consideration. Then my prices had to be compared with offers from other potential suppliers which again resulted in fresh delays and excuses for not making a final decision. This was very different from my dealings with Chinese companies when in the past I had sold J. & P. Coats products in Hong Kong where speedy decisions were a hallmark of doing business.

One afternoon I returned early from the fair and decided to relax on the rooftop garden of the hotel. I noticed a group of young men on sunbeds who were speaking in German. When I approached them we quickly disclosed our purposes of being here. It emerged that these three gentlemen were representing the well-known German steel producer Thyssen AG. When I told them about my daily visits to the fair and my frustrations about not having finalised any deal so far, they told me that they only spoke to their Chinese business partner on the first day of the fair providing them with technical specifications for their various steel products and since then they never went back to the fair but had idled away the time here on the hotel rooftop, sun bathing and playing cards. In the end they said it was all down to price. We simply go back on the last day of the fair and quote prices slightly below any offers from other producers. It had worked in the past, they said, and they were sure they would secure a contract also on this occasion. My only reply was that I wished I could share their confidence.

On return to my hotel room, my young Chinese valet gave me a letter which in perfect English invited me to participate the following afternoon on a guided tour of the General Hospital in Canton to witness the advances of Chinese medicine. Transport would be provided by the Hotel. It finished with asking me to simply confirm my availability to the Hotel receptionist. Before doing so I spoke to Ian who strongly advised me to accept this invitation as it was clearly a planned propaganda exercise aimed at demonstrating to visitors from the West the advances under a Marxist Revolutionary regime. He suggested that since my West German passport showed that my birthplace was Rostock which was located in the then still existing communist German Democratic Republic, it could be that I was selected for this guided tour because I was seen as a suitable person to speak positively about Marxist achievements on my return back home.

Whatever the reason was for my selection, the visit to the hospital was indeed a rare experience. After being given a white overall and a face mask I was invited to join the medical staff in the operating theatre. The male patient on the operating table had to be treated for a thyroid problem. With the patient appearing fully conscious, one of the doctors started inserting acupuncture needles into various part of the body and a few minutes later, with the patient remaining fully conscious, a surgeon began to cut into the area under the man's throat with virtually no blood escaping from the incision. I did not stay on to see the patient being stitched up again but as I was led away, my guide, clearly a devoted member of the Communist party, explained to me in broken English that the skills of Chinese surgery, which I had just witnessed, are of particular importance to the fighting forces of the Chinese People's Army since wounded soldiers can be treated at the front without the need to transport them back to hospitals and first aid centres. He also added that the man I had just seen on the operating table would be able to leave the hospital within the next hour and that he would be expected to return to his place of work the following day. It became clearer by the minute that this whole visit was indeed a staged propaganda exercise, as Ian had already suspected. When I asked my guide if I could buy a set of acupuncture needles to show to my friends in England he readily produced a small note which he said I should show to any taxi driver who would then take me to a pharmacy where I could collect a free set of these needles. They have remained a treasured souvenir to this very day.

The following day, following the selling technique of the three Germans, I had met on the hotel rooftop, I did not visit the fair grounds but decided go for a swim in the nearby public pool. From the entrance gate I could see that it was not terribly crowded but when I tried to purchase my entry ticket I was told in broken English that for hygiene reasons foreigners were not admitted to the pool. A strange reason for refusing me entry but then maybe the authorities feared that we polluted the water with our Western political convictions. I did not argue with the female gatekeeper and left for visiting the Canton snake market instead, stopping on route to pick up my free acupuncture needles.

The snake market turned out to be quite a gruesome set-up. There were animals I had never seen before, squeezed into appallingly narrow cages, large jars apparently containing snakes and other reptiles and an array of bird cages. A strange smell was hovering over the whole place. Judging by the large number of people in the market and the noise of traders and clients haggling over their purchases it was obvious that this was a popular source of providing Chinese kitchens with their cooking ingredients. I was hoping that the chef of the Dung Fang Hotel was not amongst the shoppers here.

With the closure of the Trade Fair now only two days away I still had not secured any contracts unlike two of my ICI colleagues who had successfully concluded their negotiations and were very satisfied with the size of business they had secured. I began to fear that I, on the other hand, might leave the fair empty-handed. On the morning of the last day, the chief negotiator of the Chinese team asked me to join them for tea. The overall atmosphere was very relaxed, almost jovial, and then it really happened. I was given an order for 400 tons of polyester tow for shipment within three months and a letter of credit drawn on the Bank of China in Hong Kong provided the financial security for the transaction. On top of all this, my Chinese negotiating partners expressed the hope that I would visit the Canton Fair again next year.

You must have felt very pleased with yourself that in the end your Canton adventure had turned out to be so successful and also to have had the opportunity to witness life in Mao Zedong's new China. Were you not given one of his famous little red books?

Thank you for mentioning it, Joseph. Yes, on our arrival at the hotel we were all given a copy of this book but I must admit that, apart from flicking through it, I did not read it at the time. Had I done so it would have given me a clue to the striking differences of Chinese people's behaviour under an authoritarian regime compared with the entrepreneurial spirit of the Chinese I had the pleasure of dealing with in my days working for J. & P. Coats in Hong Kong. Yes, I was very pleased of having had this opportunity of a brief look behind the Bamboo Curtain and who knows it might not be my last one.

The journey back to Hong Kong was comfortable and crossing the border back into the colony's territory was swift and uncomplicated. The train to Kowloon was waiting for us and filled up very quickly with people also returning from the Canton Fair.

As the train started moving down south, our group leader Ian suggested that we should treat ourselves to a small celebratory drink. A special feature of this train was a Chinese bartender, who over the years had become a well-known and much-liked celebrity. He was known as the Gin Man and during the journey he passed through each coach offering passengers drinks from a large tray held by an ornate cord round his neck. Ian must have known him from previous journeys as he was greeted like a long-lost friend when he passed our seats. The gin was served in delicate little glasses, and he promised to be back before we reached Kowloon.

Back in Kowloon we parted company and with the other three divisional representatives and Ian returning to Victoria Island, I walked the short distance back to the Peninsula Hotel. I thought to myself that a tube full of acupuncture needles and a little red book was unlikely to impress Elaine after such a long absence and that I would have to find something more imaginative for my imminent homecoming. There was always more room on her ever-growing charm bracelet and a nice piece of jade jewellery would also meet with great approval. The nearby China Emporium shop had a bewildering range of exquisite gifts in gold, precious stones and ivory where one's enthusiasm for shopping was only limited by the financial resources available.

After one more night in the Peninsula Hotel it was an early start to the airport again. The hotel management clearly paid more attention to arriving clients because now there was no Rolls Royce waiting outside the main entrance to take me to the airport. Instead the doorman hailed one of the waiting taxis and I was on my way to Kai Tak. Ever since I first set foot in Hong Kong it had amazed me how large planes like the Boeings could possibly become airborne on such a short runway which ended so abruptly at the water's edge of Hong Kong harbour. I managed to secure myself a comfortable window seat and, with the plane rising well before the end of the runway and soon swinging south over Victoria Island, I was on my long way back to the UK. I felt quite nostalgic leaving this place which after all had featured not only so much in my previous employment with J. & P. Coats but had now also allowed me to venture across the Bamboo Curtain to witness life in its mighty neighbour. How much longer will it take before this tiny and remote outpost of the Western World will succumb to the ideological pressures from its restless neighbour?

It was a joyous homecoming. During my absence Elaine had successfully widened our circle of friends which led to an ever-growing commitment to evening and weekend meetings. I was particularly pleased to learn that the family of her boss at the office, Dr Percy Carlene, had become part of our social circle. This friendship continued with three more generations of that family.

The freshly secured order from China and also the earlier positive results at the Leipzig Fair must have created the impression amongst my superiors that I was well suited to dealing with state-controlled organisations. The Soviet Union, already a customer for our polyester products, had approached ICI's Head Office in London for discussions about building a polyester plant in their country. This led to a delegation of Russian technical people arriving in Harrogate and after discussions at Crimple house, the on-site residential guesthouse of ICI Fibres Division, I had to accompany the visitors to our huge industrial complex at Wilton on Teesside. My guests seemed to be mesmerised by the sight of the seemingly endless array of pipes, smoking chimneys and blazing flares and even the haze hanging over the whole horizon was readily accepted as part of this industrial panorama. The visit proved successful, and ICI was granted a contract to build a polyester plant in a place about 200km southwest of Moscow.

A New Challenge

A sudden request from the Bulgarian State Trading Organisation to discuss supplies of polyester products resulted in an unplanned flight to Sofia, just at a time when Elaine and I had planned to take our belated annual leave. After some deliberations we arrived at a plan whereby Elaine would book a holiday in the vicinity of Athens where I would then join her after concluding my discussions in Sofia. After a quick weekend trip to Scotland to have Elaine's mother look after our dog Mitzi, our holiday plan was put into action and a booking was made at a hotel just north of Athen's airport with secluded beach facilities nearby.

On reflection I should have asked our Greek agent to check out the suitability of the hotel chosen by the UK travel agent because when I arrived at the hotel Elaine's welcome was rather muted. Before I could ask any questions the answer became noisily clear as a huge aircraft was just skimming over the roof of the hotel. It immediately reminded me of the approach to Kai Tak Airport in Hong Kong. Thankfully, Elaine explained, there were no incoming flights after 10 pm the previous night but it started again very early in the morning. As we had not intended to spend the day in the hotel anyway, we decided to keep it as our holiday location, enjoy the nearby beachside and hire a car to visit other beaches and numerous historical sites. It all turned into an enjoyable and interesting holiday.

After retrieving our dog from Scotland, life in the office had by no means ceased to spring surprises on me. During my absence the company had been approached by the Czechoslovakian Embassy in London, asking if ICI could hold a fashion show in Prague to highlight the applications and fashion aspects of their Crimplene yarns. Over the years I have been involved in a number of odd jobs but organising a fashion show would certainly be a new challenge. And on top of this, it would be in a country behind the Iron Curtain where one could probably not resort to help from Western professional agencies. My manager and the export director, Mr Harris, both thought that this was a good sign given the unexpected opportunity to promote our product in an Iron Curtain country with the possible prospect of receiving similar requests from neighbouring Eastern Bloc states. When I was told that the show would be expected before year-end I knew that a pressurised few weeks lay ahead. I was promised that our advertising manager would be at my full disposal and our marketing people would identify UK clothing manufacturers who have Crimplene garments on their existing selling ranges. In addition, it was agreed that the company would purchase a van to transport the garments to Prague. When I saw that the company would mobilise all possible resources to help me in this unusual venture, I began to feel increasingly confident and was quite looking forward to masterminding such a show. The prospect of having a front seat at such an event began to appeal to me more and more.

Earlier in the year, recognising that my territorial remit was so large that I would spend literally most of my time flying from country to country, the Harrogate Management had decided to appoint a liaison officer to help me in two of the Eastern Bloc countries namely Czechoslovakia and Hungary. He was located in ICI's main office in Vienna and his name was Reinhold Bethusy. This now proved to be an invaluable support in getting my Crimplene fashion show off the ground. I telephoned Reinhold, briefed him on the forthcoming event and asked him to travel immediately to Prague to check out suitable venues and above all to find a local agency that could provide attractive models, both female and male and the all-important catwalk. Three days later Reinhold phoned back to inform me that with magnificent help from the commercial attaché at the UK Embassy in Prague, all the local preparations for the show were in place and that an open-ended permit for our Crimplene van to enter Czechoslovakia had been secured. All he needed to know now was the date on which we hoped to stage this Crimplene spectacle to enable him to mobilise the local state-controlled press and radio to ensure a maximum attendance.

And so, on 1st October, at a small farewell gathering outside the main entrance of our Harrogate offices, attended also by our director, Mr Harris, the van, covered on all sides with the message 'Crimplene for Everyone' was ready for its long journey to Prague. The driver was a young man, Allan Baines, who only recently had joined the Export Department as a junior clerk. To share the driving, a member of the Advertising Department was to accompany him. Laden with an amazing array of ladies and gents Crimplene garments and the necessary visas for the drivers, the van finally left the site.

The following day I booked my flight to Prague to assist Reinhold in the final preparations for the show and to familiarise myself with the hall he had booked for the event. It was in an impressive-looking hotel in central Prague and was probably a ballroom in pre-communist days. Two days later the Crimplene van arrived and we fixed the date for the actual show with Reinhold now providing details to the media channels.

Everything seemed to function like clockwork. In a

quickly arranged rehearsal the female models and the one male model ensured that the garments brought by the Crimplene van were of the right fit. A variety of headgear and accessories was chosen and on top of all this the local model agency provided a young male bilingual presenter to first help me with my opening address but also with introducing the modelled garments to the hopefully large crowd attending the show.

And then it all really happened. A trickle of people quickly turned into a queue of well-dressed people entering the hotel. In the reception area, hotel staff were lined up to receive guests with an offering of canapés and Krim Sekt. I mingled for a while with the incoming crowd and was pleased to see that virtually all the Eastern Bloc embassies in Prague had sent a delegate to our show. I had hoped that our own UK ambassador would make a brief appearance at the show to highlight the close commercial links between the two countries but then his commitment to impartiality probably made it difficult for him to attend an ICI-sponsored event. I was very pleased however when Reinhold introduced me to the commercial attaché of the UK Embassy who had been so supportive of our endeavours.

After my opening speech, kept to short phrases to allow the interpreter to repeat them in the Czech language, I finally took my centre seat in the front row and watched these very attractive girls demonstrate their presentational skills. One of the models clearly tried to attract my personal attention by giving me a rather surreptitious smile every time she passed in front of me on the catwalk.

I felt I had really reached a highpoint in my professional life. Will it from now on be back to the decidedly less glamorous task of selling polyester and nylon yarns to people whose main ambition it was to argue over prices and conditions and sometimes even in a hostile and abusive manner? And yet, I cannot deny that in that line of work there have also been moments of great joy and satisfaction when securing a sizeable sales contract or forming new relationships.

Do I detect in your comments that your success in Prague could possibly make you seek a role in the obviously more glamorous world of fashion?

No, Joseph, I do not think so. Yes, Prague was a wonderful experience but in the end I could not see it as a job for the longer term. There was also the lure to see many more of the countries in my existing job portfolio. Prior to my departure for Prague, my export director, Mr Harris, had already indicated that more business opportunities should be explored in East and West Africa. He also promised to accompany me the following year on some of my visits to Eastern Bloc countries.

In December I did my round of courtesy visits to East European embassies in London. There were some delicate moments when the spectacular escape of the spy George Blake from Dartmoor Prison was gleefully mentioned on two occasions. Little did I know at that stage how this event would impact on my own future career in ICI. In Scotland we once again enjoyed the traditional hospitality during the festive season, and as a special treat we decided to trade in our Austin Morris for a gleaming new car, a Singer model, which is rarely seen on the roads these days.

To start the new year, I visited the important textile manufacturing centre of Sabadell in northern Spain. Accompanied by our ICI fibres representative, Peter Boath, we devoted this visit mainly to increasing our sales of nylon yarns to the country's leading manufacturers of net curtains and other forms of netting.

Having hardly set foot again in Harrogate, a request arrived to come to Budapest for negotiations on fresh polyester tow deliveries and also to visit the Ministry of Telecommunications. Rumours had circulated in the office for some time that the product development people had been working on creating a cable rope consisting of a strong polyester yarn core covered in a PVC mantle. The intended application was to replace steel wires supporting high freestanding masts as required for radio, telephone and television transmissions. The Hungarians were clearly interested in learning more about this possible replacement of steel wires and it fell to me to enlighten them in a field where I was a complete novice. Equipped with samples and literature, I presented myself to the Ministry and in answering their rather technical questions I tried to sound as knowledgeable as I possibly could. It was in fact two years later that a new mast was erected with support from this ICI product.

In the years to come I always enjoyed my visits to Budapest. The people in the State Trading Organisation were friendly and welcoming, the cafes reminded one of the well-known coffee houses in Vienna and an evening meal at Mathyas Pinces Restaurant was always an unforgettable experience, spiced up by the violinists going from table to table to entrance the guests with their traditional music. On top of all this there was the captivating spectacle of the Danube river flanked on both sides by architectural gems, a reminder of the city's past importance in the Austro-Hungarian days.

Back home, my hopes of getting time to prepare for my visits to Africa suffered a setback when Mr Harris asked me to accompany him on a visit to Greece. I learnt that our agent Mr Gyftopolos had started to build a plant for the production of Crimplene yarns somewhere south of Athens and that he was seeking ICI's participation in this venture. On our arrival in Athens our agent first took us to his large retail shop in the centre of the city to meet also his mother. It became clear immediately that she was the dominant member of the Gyftopolos family and that her son would always be guided by her decisions. Whilst we were in the shop, the mother never left her place behind a noisy old cash register, taking money from customers in spite of other staff being readily available. After a short and rather serious discussion between mother and son, we finally set off on our trip to the new factory site. During the journey her son admitted that when it comes to money his mother only trusted herself. He also admitted that his mother had not allowed him to get married until after his elder sister had found a partner for life.

With a two-hour drive ahead of us and daylight fading, our agent suggested that we spend the night in a hotel in a place called Nafplio near to his factory on the other side of the bay in a village called Mili. This trip also gave me the opportunity to cast a quick glance at the famous Corinth Canal.

On our visit to Mili the following day we discovered the factory was still only a semi-finished project. The building was completed but the machinery was still unpacked in large crates, and it became clear that it would take a few more weeks if not months before it would become operational, also taking into account that personnel had to be hired and trained.

The suggestion of Mr Gyftopolos to have ICI as a partner in this venture was met with a muted response from Mr Harris. As a compromise he offered that ICI would stand as a guarantor for some of the short-term loans already taken out by our agent and that favourable terms would be offered for polyester yarn supplies once the factory became operational. Although not meeting his original expectations, our agent accepted it as a compromise solution. We all hoped that after our return to Athens his mother would concur with our agreement.

As time went by, our business relationship with Greece really flourished and on his occasional visits to Harrogate Mr Gyftopolos always enjoyed the special attention extended to him by Mr Harris.

On our return to Harrogate, I had really hoped to get some time to prepare for my forthcoming trip to Africa but the 'Crimplene Revolution' had reached such a momentum that normal planning processes were swept aside. My old friend and mentor Mike Miliangos who had organised my first return behind the Iron Curtain informed us that he had also joined the bandwagon of Crimplene enthusiasts and had purchased a factory in Switzerland already equipped with machinery to produce Crimplene yarns. He would welcome the visit of an ICI technician and would be pleased if I could also be available. When I looked up the map to establish the location of his factory, I noticed it was near Geneva. The hope of a quick dash across the border to see my mother in Freiburg therefore had to be abandoned. The manufacturing plant turned out to be an example of Swiss precision engineering, clean and airy and surrounded by well-tended lawns and flower beds with the staff dressed in smart-looking overalls. I was not surprised when Mike told me that he was hoping to sell a large part of his future production to countries behind the Iron Curtain, possibly in barter deals, a form of trading I had become involved in myself but in which Mike seemed to excel.

Southern Skies

With entry visas required for all the African countries I was planning to visit, my West German passport had to be sent to their London-based embassies. This had the welcome side effect that for nearly a fortnight I did not have to rush off to airports and instead could enjoy the comfort of regular office hours. We went for outings in the evenings with friends and colleagues to the well-known Squinting Cat Pub and other watering holes around Harrogate and we also entertained guests at our Knaresborough home. On top of all this Elaine and I took an extra day off work to visit her mother in Elderslie. Unfortunately this journey was marred by an accident on our return from Scotland. As we were travelling southwards on the A1 highway on our final approach to Knaresborough a motorcar came out of a minor side road and hit the rear end of our new Singer car. The offending vehicle did not even stop, crossed the highway and disappeared in the distance. Feeling quite shocked, neither Elaine or I could even remember the type of the offending vehicle nor was I sure of its colour. We drove on to the next petrol station where I telephoned the police to report the unfortunate incidence. An inspection of the rear of the car also showed that the colour of the hit and run driver's vehicle must have been deep red according to the paint scrapings. Strangely enough it was about two years later that our car insurance company informed us that the police had traced the reckless driver and his vehicle.

With my passport full of visas, the day had finally arrived for my departure to Africa. First stop Nairobi. For representation in the East African countries of Kenya,

Uganda and Tanzania, ICI, after having discontinued its own direct presence in Nairobi in 1949, had entered into a close relationship with the local company, Twiga Chemicals. This was a highly respected and diversified enterprise but whilst actively promoting ICI's business in the more traditional sectors like dyestuffs, paints, pharmaceuticals and other products, no active work had been done to seek also business opportunities for ICI's youngest division in Harrogate. This lack of interaction with Harrogate was obviously the reason why my export director had suddenly seen the urgency to send me on this mission. After discussions with the Twiga Chemicals Management, it was decided to allocate one more person to the already existing ICI Department in Twiga Chemicals and that that person would be available to give full assistance for the duration of my visit and above all seek business opportunities thereafter.

The candidate for this position was a middle-aged gentleman who I was told had held a senior position in the previous colonial civil service in Kenya. He introduced himself as Kevin. I would have preferred a person with some knowledge of the textile industry but I had to accept what was offered to me. During a brief courtesy visit to the ICI Department, I was introduced also to a young lady whose responsibility was the dyestuffs business, which was primarily with the textile industry in East Africa. She was a lady with an outgoing personality, enthusiastic and familiar with the textile industry. She was clearly the type of helper I would have preferred to get our polyester and nylon business off to a good start. I was very pleased when she offered to give the candidate nominated for our business her full support. I must have left quite a favourable impression with her because before leaving the office she asked me if I was free on Sunday to join her and her family for dinner at their home. I thanked her for such an instant and friendly gesture to a stranger she had never met before. She said, call it a welcome to Nairobi.

And so, equipped with a bunch of flowers, I turned up at their bungalow house not far from the city centre. It was a truly enjoyable evening, not just the meal but also the conversations with the lady's husband and their two teenage daughters. It gave me a quick insight into life in Kenya and also a clearer understanding of the troubled times in the recent past. If during my stay in Kenya I could free myself for half a day they suggested that I visit the nearby Nairobi National Park and enjoy the thrill of a mini safari.

Whilst my nominated helper and future fibres representative had no knowledge of the textile industry he had a remarkably good knowledge of where the important enterprises were located. Over a large map of East Africa, we devised a travelling programme for the next six days which would take us as far east as Kampala in Uganda and then west again to Mombasa on the Indian Ocean.

If you do not mind my saying so but listening to all this makes one feel you are having an African holiday at your employer's expense.

You are probably not too far off the mark, Joseph. As you know from earlier revelations to you, I have had the good fortune of firstly having worked for a company who had already whetted my appetite for travelling by sending me to the USA and Australia and now my new employer has entrusted me with responsibilities stretching from China and Europe to Africa.

In all my travels I have always given top priority to serving the interests of my employer but whenever the opportunity arose, I have also tried to widen my own personal horizon of the places I was fortunate enough to visit. I felt sure that back in Harrogate my export director would not have denied me a brief visit to a safari park.

This visit, in fact, took place much earlier than I had expected when my helper suggested that we do it the following day before setting off east for our commercial tour.

And so in the morning we drove into the park in the Twiga company car. Very soon we were surrounded by monkeys who were clearly accustomed to cars and visitors and did not hesitate to sit in front of us on the car bonnet staring at us and even pulling the windscreen wipers for their own amusement. Soon we spotted a herd of majestic giraffes. Zebras and two rhinos appeared out of nowhere but it took another hour before we came across a pride of lions. My helper drove the car right up to where the lions were resting which led to some of them rising and surrounding our car. Suddenly we heard a crunching noise at the back of the car and we both agreed that it was high time to leave the lions behind us.

When finally leaving the park, we discovered that the cover of one of the rear lights was missing and we blamed the lion for that. With a replacement car from Twiga, we finally set off east with our first stop at Naivasha where Kevin had already booked our hotel rooms. On our approach to Naivasha I had already noticed the large lake which seemed to be teeming with bird life. "Tomorrow," Kevin said, "you will see a lot more when we get to Nakuru. There, thousands of flamingos will make the lake look red."

Nakuru was a town much larger than I had expected. It had a European feel to it, with streets lined by shops and hotels and an astonishing volume of modern-day traffic. On our approach I had already noticed the promised spectacle of countless flamingos giving the lake a reddish tinge and also some larger animals standing in the shallow water. Kevin gave me some background information on Nakuru and its history as the gateway into the White Highlands of Kenya. As we drove along it soon became clear that this town was also a very important diversified industrial centre, and I was looking forward to my first visit to an African factory. With no prior arrangements having been made for our visit I was impressed how the presentation of our Twiga and ICI visiting cards led to almost instant access to the senior management of the company, two gentlemen of Indian descent. They admitted that they had already been watching the modern trend of blending cotton with polyester fibre and that they had done a trial in their spinning mill. They were waiting to hear from one of their customers, a local weaving company, how the blended yarns had performed on their looms. Since this customer was also in Nakuru, they suggested that we should visit them as well. And this we did. On arrival we were met like long-lost friends and as we quickly discovered they had been longstanding customers for ICI's textile dyestuffs. The weaving trials with the blended yarns had been successful, we were told, but they had not yet completed the colouring trials of the finished cloth. Once again, the senior staff were of Indian descent, a feature repeated on a few more occasions during my travels in both East and later also in West Africa. Overall, the omens for a first sale in Nakuru looked promising and indeed a first order was placed after I had left Kenya. Our second call was on a company producing all kinds of netting. They already purchased nylon yarns from one of our European competitors but requested samples in various deniers for new product developments. We finished our stay in Nakuru with a visit to another large cotton spinning mill. Their management left us in no doubt, that they wished to remain a pure cotton processor which they maintained was more appropriate for the climatic conditions of equatorial

Africa. I was supposed to convince them of the benefits of polyester but deep down, when exposed to the midday heat and the high humidity, I had to admit that a pure cotton shirt had its advantages.

As we were about to leave Nakuru, Kevin suddenly felt very unwell and suggested to visit the local hospital for a check-up. It was a very modern-looking set-up. Kevin was promptly seen by a doctor who established that he had not only a high degree of fever but also a very low blood pressure and he suspected also a bowel blockage. He suggested that Kevin returned immediately to Nairobi where a more thorough test could be carried out. I offered to drive Kevin back immediately but he insisted that it would be quicker by train. The hospital staff informed us that there were only two train services to Nairobi per day but if we rushed to the station we might still be able to catch the afternoon departure. By the time we reached the station, Kevin seemed to have recovered a little. We discovered that the next train departure was almost imminent and judging by the number of travellers already in the coaches this was clearly a popular form of travel to visit Kenya's capital city.

We managed to find a seat for Kevin but with the train beginning to move I had to disembark swiftly. My next stop was the local main post office to telephone the Twiga office to ensure that someone would go and meet Kevin off this train and take him to the Nairobi Hospital. The Twiga manager offered to send a junior employee to accompany me for the rest of my journey but I thanked him for his offer and assured him that I am not unfamiliar with disruptions and unforeseen setbacks and that I would proceed on my own.

And on this note I finally left Nakuru heading further west to Kisumu. Now I had to do all the driving myself.

Large numbers of trucks and also agricultural vehicles slowed down my driving and when I finally reached the outskirts of Kisumu road signs alerted me that this town was also the home of a large port, in fact one of the largest ones on Lake Victoria.

Kisumu itself was a bustling township with modern-looking shopping alleys interspersed with colourful street markets and also an impressive-looking railway station. Before Kevin had to be transported back to Nairobi, he had already told me that he had selected the Sovereign Hotel for our stay in Kisumu. I was received with great courtesy, which, as I learnt later from the receptionist, was probably due to past visits of other representatives of the Twiga organisation. The hotel still had decor which did not hide its colonial past.

A brief visit to the port area revealed a busy harbour with several medium-sized barges being loaded with crates and sacks and driven on by locals, shouting and waving sticks, a small herd of goats was forced onto one of the boats. I could have spent hours watching the hustle and bustle of this place which, although being an inland port on a large lake, had the atmosphere of a real seaside harbour.

The Kisumu Cotton Mill turned out to be a sizeable enterprise with several buildings spread over a fenced-in compound. The manager was a gentleman originally from Wiltshire and when I told him that I had done my training in cotton spinning in the mills of my previous employer J. & P. Coats in Paisley an instant rapport was established between us. Not surprisingly, the manager was very informed about the modern trend of blending cotton with man-made fibres but admitted that due to the preferences of his local customers his mill had so far only produced pure cotton yarns. However, he added my arrival was very timely, because his company had received requests from some European weavers for blended yarns and that he had been thinking already of conducting some trials. Also, he said supplies from their local cotton suppliers, who were mainly small holdings that depended on cotton as a cash crop, had been erratic lately and also of variable quality. After placing a trial order and offering some refreshments he insisted on a walk through the spinning mill where I was greeted with the high-pitched noise I so well remembered from my own training days in Scotland. I alerted him to the need for a blending battery and promised to send him the name of a UK supplier as soon as I returned to the UK. On my departure, the manager made some helpful suggestions on the choice of roads for my imminent journey to Jinja and how to deal with the formalities of crossing into Uganda. I really enjoyed my visit to Kisumu. Will I ever come back again?

The journey to Jinja took me through a large variety of landscapes. Forests, plantations (which I later discovered were tea plantations) and numerous villages and settlements with cultivated fields stretching out on either side of the road. Most reassuringly, some of those villages also had petrol stations.

The border crossing at a town called Busia was a remarkably uncomplicated affair, despite the gentle warnings I was given by the manager in Kisumu. A smartly uniformed official gave my visa a brief glance, then stamped my passport and wished me a good onward journey to Jinja.

According to Kevin's travel programme, my next stay was in a place called Coronation Park, just outside the main township on the western bank of the lake and the beginning of the River Nile. This was a particularly welcome choice as it was near to a monument in which my friend and best man Alex Maitland had expressed a special interest. He was in the process of writing a book about the explorer John Hanning Speke who was credited with having found the origin of the River Nile and Alex had asked me to procure a picture of this monument. With instructions from the hotel staff, I quickly found the monument and on my return I purchased a postcard in the hotel, the image of which eventually appeared in Alex's publication.

After crossing the bridge over the Nile my next call was to a large cotton spinning mill right on the western bank of the river. In size and dimension it almost equalled the factory I had just left in Kisumu but this one was under Indian management. Again, I was cordially welcomed by the general manager who informed me that the mill was British owned and that a large portion of their production was sent to England via the Kenyan port of Mombasa. The British mill owners had already indicated recently to make further investments to enable the production of cotton/polyester blended yarns which had gained rapid popularity with English weavers and garment makers. I was assured that when the processing lines had been set up, ICI's polyester fibre would be the preferred product. Whilst sitting in the general manager's office our conversation was suddenly interrupted by a loud noise of metal hitting metal just outside the building. "They are our regular visitors," the general manager said. "It is a group of hippos who for some unknown reason appear almost daily and like to rummage around in our backyard where we keep discarded machinery and other obsolete equipment." A look out of the office window confirmed his remarks and it was certainly the closest I ever got to live hippos.

My most eastern destination was the capital of Uganda, Kampala, and although only a relatively short distance from

Jinja my driving was frequently slowed down by agricultural vehicles, herds of cows and goats, groups of pedestrians carrying baskets and sacks and the odd broken down car. I was beginning to get quite anxious about my slow progress because according to the original travel schedule I had to make one more call on another large textile enterprise just outside Kampala. After that I was to return the car to the local Twiga office in Kampala and collect from them my flight ticket for my return to Nairobi late afternoon. Time was not on my side and the prospect of including some sightseeing was very slim.

The gated entrance to the factory grounds and also the appearance of the buildings gave an instant impression of a well-run and prosperous business. Again my ICI and Twiga business card ensured a welcoming reception but what struck me most was the wonderful cool air provided by an obviously highly efficient air-conditioning system. It must have been the coolest office I had ever encountered during my African trip. I was told that the Hinduja Group, which also owned this factory, was a longstanding customer for various ICI products, not only in East Africa but worldwide. With several of their key customers being in the UK they were well aware of the vogue for polyester/cotton blended fabrics and plans were already in hand to install the extra equipment for making blended yarns in the near future. I was assured that ICI will be the preferred supplier and that an order will be placed shortly via the local Twiga office. This having been my last call, I felt quite satisfied with the overall outcome in Uganda.

After returning my car to the Twiga office and collecting my flight ticket to Nairobi I even found time to visit a street market to buy myself a souvenir. A painter artist drew my particular attention. Amongst his displays was a small oil painting on canvas, depicting a lakeside scene with a typical tropical background. It still adorns our home today.

The flight back to Nairobi was uneventful, lasting only just over one hour. As I found out the following day, Kevin had fully recovered from his illness and was ready to accompany me on my final journey east ending in Mombasa. When the Twiga manager asked me to see him under four eyes I was wondering if I had committed any faux pas during my travels. As it turned out, he had received a telephone call from ICI's London office to put a specific request to me. Once finished with my work in Kenya would I be willing to make an additional trip to Rhodesia as I was still a citizen of West Germany, carried a West German passport and was thus not restricted from entering this country, embargoed by the UK following the Unilateral Declaration of Independence by Mr Ian Smith in 1965. Rhodesia was an important market for a variety of ICI products, particularly for the mining industry, dyestuffs, pharmaceuticals and agriculture and the company was concerned that their inability to supply their traditional customers would lead to other international competitors taking over the business. Apparently the Salisbury office had been able to draw on some token supplies from ICI in Johannesburg in neighbouring South Africa but, whilst not putting me under any compulsion, it was suggested that if I were to travel to Salisbury I could possibly help the local staff to improve the supply situation.

If you do not mind my saying so, but it looks to me that you are in effect being asked to help minimise the effect of a government-imposed blockade of that country. Considering that as a foreigner, requiring a permit to work and live in the UK, did you not feel this was too risky a mission to undertake? From what I have read in the press the UK government is very serious about this blockade and have even stationed a warship outside the harbour off Maputo in neighbouring Mozambique to stop goods from reaching Rhodesia.

I am not surprised by your critical observation, Joseph, but as you must have gathered by now I have always enjoyed facing up to challenges. The history books are full of incidences where the power of commerce has led to war-hungry politicians being forced to seek compromises. Just look at the example of the Hanseatic League stretching from Russia to the UK which allowed trade and human relationships to flourish whilst rulers and politicians were often at each other's throat. In any case, I felt sure that if anything went wrong, ICI would not let me down.

I informed the Twiga manager to let London know that I would make the requested visit after completing my commercial programme in Kenya. To avoid a long and time-consuming car journey to Mombasa and taking into account that we had only three firms targeted for our visit, it was decided that Kevin and I would go by air. The local Twiga office was to provide transport and arrange our accommodation for one night.

The flight of just over one hour was far too short for my liking. Having secured a window seat and the plane flying at relative low altitude, I enjoyed looking at the countryside below me and above all I got a wonderful view of the majestic, snow-capped Kilimanjaro Mountain.

On our arrival, everything happened like clockwork. A young Twiga employee drove us to the companies we had marked out to visit. They were large textile conglomerates and whilst we were not able to secure any orders we were asked to send a variety of samples of our polyester and nylon products. With all three enterprises already being long-standing customers of ICI's Dyestuffs Division we felt sure that we could also become a supplier in the not-too-distant future. Kevin, who appeared to be quite familiar with Mombasa and its surroundings, insisted that we also pay a brief visit to the nearby beaches, the target of tourists from all over Europe. They were indeed magnificent stretches of sandy coastline but I thought to myself that the wonderful dunes and endless stretches of golden sand I so enjoyed on the Baltic Sea in my own childhood days could hold their own with what I saw here. One distinctive difference was that on my childhood beaches one was not repeatedly approached by beach vendors trying to sell you sunglasses, lotions, beads and wood carvings. On our way back to the hotel, our young Twiga driver gave us a sightseeing tour through Mombasa, culminating in a drive down a wide twin-lane boulevard flanked by four gigantic images of elephant tusks. Mombasa appeared to have a decidedly more multicultural atmosphere than Nairobi and being Kenya's major seaport it was a hub of great activity. I was hoping that this would not be my only ever visit to this city.

Back in Nairobi, preparations had already been made for me to fly to Rhodesia the next day. I was advised that on arrival in Salisbury I should ask the local immigration officer not to stamp my West German passport to avoid repercussions on my eventual return to the UK.

On 17th of April, after a three-hour flight, the Air Ethiopia plane landed in Salisbury International Airport. I had no problems in persuading the immigration officer not to stamp my passport and in the arrival hall I was greeted by a young man from the local ICI office by the name of Ian who looked like the younger version of the country's leader, Mr Ian Smith. To my surprise, young Ian told me that during my visit I would be staying at his house. As it turned out it was actually his parents' house, a very spacious and elegant villa on the outskirts of the town.

Considering that in the past Rhodesia had been one of the key African markets for ICI, the local office appeared to be quite modest with only a handful of staff members. The manager gave me a full description of the present supply problems. Until recently, neighbouring Mozambique had been a productive route for obtaining some supplies but with the increased British blockade of that country such deliveries had now been reduced to a trickle. It was important now to seek more help from the other friendly neighbouring state of South Africa which was more immune to any blockading attempts. The main areas of concern were pharmaceutical products, chemicals for the important mining industry and dyestuffs for the wide range of textiles processors. The final conclusion was that we would approach a number of Salisbury-based import houses with the request to make purchases on our behalf from South African distributors of ICI products and then to put these imported goods back at our disposal in Salisbury, after compensating the importer for his efforts. In a telephone call with the ICI office in Johannesburg, they expressed their full support and promised to forward details of their key distributors of various ICI products. The next step was to identify and contact the major import/export firms in Salisbury to see if they would collaborate with us. The following day the office manager and I visited three such firms and their response to our proposal was not only very positive but revealed that they were already actively involved in trans-border trade with South Africa. With staff in the ICI Office now left in charge of dealing with the details of future transactions, my host Ian suggested that I should use my unexpected stopover in his country to visit the spectacular Victoria Falls which were only an hour's flight away from Salisbury and which even in these troubled times remained a major tourist attraction.

I was delighted with his suggestion. There were regular flights to and from the Falls which allowed me to make it a day trip. Even the approach to the Victoria Falls Airport presented me with a colourful spectacle. The early morning sun gave the rising spray from the Falls the impression of a large rainbow-coloured cloud. It was a sight to remember. After a quick breakfast in the nearby Victoria Falls Hotel, I found a good vantage point to watch this aqueous spectacle close by, listen to the roaring sound and get profoundly drenched in the ever-present spray clouds. A walk on the Falls bridge, connecting Rhodesia with Zambia, gave me the opportunity to marvel also at the upper region of the Zambesi River and the majestic and seemingly endless canyon at the foot of the Falls. In the end, time was up to return to the airport for my flight back to Salisbury.

The time had come for me to plan my return to the UK. After exploring various exit routes, it emerged that flying first to Johannesburg would be the quickest way back to London. Rerouting myself back via Johannesburg also had a very personal attraction for me because it gave me an opportunity to visit my brother Lothar whom I had not seen for many years and who now resided with his wife Erika in Johannesburg. The Air Rhodesia Viscount plane was very comfortable with excellent inflight service. It was also very informative because the gentleman sitting next to me and who came from Bulawayo entertained me with a vivid description of the current problems in his country, the feuding amongst the tribal factions and the efforts by the government to maintain some form of civil order. It made the four-hour flight pass very quickly.

My passage through the immigration control was trouble-free and friendly but all this changed into a mini drama when I reached the baggage hall to collect my suitcase. When the baggage was wheeled into the hall on large trollies a middle-aged lady of dark complexion but possibly of Indian descent struggled very much to retrieve her rather oversized suitcase. Without giving the matter further thought, I rushed over to give her a helping hand. When minutes later I made my way through the exit channel, two uniformed officers asked me to follow them to an adjacent small room, where I was told that I had disregarded the apartheid regulations which was a punishable offence resulting in a substantial fine or a judicial procedure. Needless to say, I was infuriated by this form of welcome in South Africa. I had heard and read about the country's policy of colour segregation but could not believe that a simple act of physical assistance, which in any civil society would have been regarded as an act of courtesy, could lead to a fine or even imprisonment. My own cash resources had by now dwindled to a level where I had just enough money left to pay for my return flight to the UK. I certainly did not want my brother to become involved in this unfortunate matter and in the end I asked for permission to phone the local ICI office to seek their assistance. The office manager with whom we had only spoken days before from Salisbury asked me to hand over the telephone to one of the officers and after two or three minutes the telephone was handed back to me and I learnt that a bail-out fine would be paid by the ICI office on my behalf and that it had been agreed that I would be free to leave the airport. On my way out I passed a row of airline offices and when I saw the BOAC one I decided there and then to purchase my return ticket to London and Yeadon for the following day. Outside the building I made sure to take the Whites-only bus into Johannesburg. It was early evening before I found my brother's apartment in a high-rise tenement building in the centre of the city. Not having seen each other for a number of years and with both of us also having been rather economical with exchanging letters it turned into a wonderful reunion, bringing us up to date on happenings in the wider family and seeing also for the first time the latest addition, my baby nephew Michael.

After a comfortable overnight stay I returned to the airport and boarded my plane to the UK with stopovers in Nairobi and Rome. In London, my passage through the immigration control was a mere routine procedure and on reaching the transit lounge I made the long overdue telephone call to the office to speak to Elaine. It was wonderful to hear her voice again and to learn that all was well at home. I gave her details of my arrival in Yeadon and she promised to organise a company car to collect me. It was a comforting feeling to be home again.

That evening we celebrated my return with a lavish meal at our favourite restaurant down on the banks of the River Nidd in Knaresborough. Elaine gave me an update on happenings in the office and up north in Scotland, adding that her mother had asked for an early convenient date to pay us a visit. I reminded Elaine that I still had to complete my African tour by also visiting West Africa and that it would therefore be better to delay a decision on her mother's visit until I was back from there. When Elaine asked how long my next trip would last I could sense a feeling of disappointment and it came not as a complete surprise when she added, "Just as well I have a dog to keep me company." Even my assurances that future business commitments would be mainly in Europe with short absences did not fully lift the cloud over what I had hoped to be a more joyful reunion on my return.

Surely, Elaine must have been aware that your work in an export department of a major national company would lead to a life with repeated and sometimes also quite long separations. From what you have told me before, long separations were already a hallmark of your drawn-out courtship.

Your observations are absolutely right, Joseph. The difference was that in our courtship days Elaine had the company and support of her mother. Thankfully we now had been able to build up a wider circle of friends and acquaintances here in Harrogate who could be relied upon in moments of need. Then there was also her own daily work at the office which provided her with mental stimulus and also a better understanding of the demands and complexities of a worldwide business. And indeed, as time progressed Elaine developed a more philosophical attitude to my unavoidable journeys abroad. When meeting up with friends or the wider family and discussing recent or past local events, Elaine often dropped the remark that once again on that particular occasion, "I had shone with my absence."

A day after having submitted my report on my East Africa visit the export manager called me to inform me that our director, Mr Harris, would like to see us both to review my forthcoming trip to Nigeria and Ghana. This did not come as a complete surprise since a number of reports in the British press had mentioned the growing unrest between tribal factions in Nigeria and a general atmosphere of political instability throughout the country. I thought to myself that this meeting with our director was probably called to tell me that the trip should be cancelled.

Before even mentioning the issue of West Africa, Mr Harris informed us that he had received a letter from the Soviet State Trading Organisation in London with an invitation to visit their Moscow-based import and export company Exportljon to discuss the supply of polyester fibre and tow and to time such a visit preferably for the end of May. Mr Harris clearly regarded this as a major business opportunity far outweighing the opportunities envisaged in Africa. I had expected him to conclude that my trip to West Africa should now be put on hold but to my surprise he said that I should go ahead but to make sure I was back before the end of May to accompany him on the trip to Moscow. He added that he had consulted ICI's Head Office in London and also his counterparts in other ICI divisions with business interests in Nigeria who had all reassured him that despite the reported unrest in the country business relationships had continued as normal.

On 8th of May, a day forever engrained in my memory as the day the war in Europe came to an end in 1945 and the outgoing dictatorship was replaced with a new one, I finally set off on my nine-hour flight to Lagos. The officers at the passport and baggage control greeted me with a friendly smile and the whole passage through the airport was smooth and efficient. Certainly no sign of any underlying tension or hostility to foreigners. Outside the building a crowd of colourfully dressed taxi drivers were offering their services to the new arrivals. One of them, clearly more enterprising than his colleagues, came straight to me, grabbed my suitcase and pointed to one of the nearby stationed cars.

My pre-booked hotel was in the centre of Lagos and the ride from the airport left me in no doubt that this was a large and wealthy city with well-known European and American brand names being promoted profusely.

The receptionist at the hotel told me that they were honoured to have me following a long tradition of visits from gentlemen from ICI. Having received my room keys, I headed for the lift door when I was overtaken by two strangely dressed young men heading for the same lift entrance. They wore long zipped-up boots and were dressed in what looked like overalls with lots of small pockets. There were just the three of us in the lift but as we ascended I found to my surprise that the two young men were taking to each other in German and above all in the distinct accent of Saxony, so familiar to me since my mother hailed from that part of Germany and which was now part of the communist GDR. During the short trip in the lift, I did not make myself known to them as a fellow German but when I mentioned it the next day to the ICI office manager he threw some more light on the matter. He explained that rumours are circulating that the present federal government had hired pilots from East Germany to train their own less-experienced pilots and even to carry out missions on their own against tribal dissidents.

I laid out my own itinerary for the next four days with the most easterly point being the township of Enugu. "It is a good day's journey from here," the manager stressed, "and you need an experienced driver." He called in a very young-looking member of staff who introduced himself as Bako. When he was told of my planned visit to Enugu his initial enthusiasm of becoming my driver faded quite visibly. "I am a Yoruba," he explained, "and travelling to Enugu which is in the tribal heartland of the Igbo people could expose me to all sorts of maltreatment." It was only thanks to the reassurances from the office manager that the presence of a European co-traveller would ensure his personal safety that Bako finally agreed to be my driver.

The following morning we set off for our journey into the unknown. Bako spoke English fluently and he took great pride in explaining the countryside to me as we were heading east on what was clearly an important arterial road. Our first stop was at Benin City where I wanted to visit a large cotton spinning mill, already a customer of ICI's Dyestuffs Division. As we approached the outskirts of Benin City, I had noticed the large plantations of palm oil trees. Even the spinning mill seemed to be surrounded by orderly rows of these trees and I was not surprised when Bako explained to me that this was the major centre of palm oil production in Nigeria.

On our last stretch to the mill, Bako drew my attention to large black clouds appearing on the horizon to which he added that within an hour we would have a massive tropical downpour. And he was right.

The mill manager acknowledged that he was aware of the growing importance of cotton/polyester blended yarns and that the mill owners had already been approached to sanction the capital needed for the additional machinery. "When we are ready," he added, "we shall inform your office in Lagos."

As we left the mill compound it had already started to rain but suddenly the skies seemed to open up requiring Bako to drive at snail's pace. "There is no point in heading further east today," he said, "better to seek shelter in Benin City and continue our journey in the morning. It will be a fine day again." With the windscreen wipers struggling to cope with the torrential downpour we stopped at the first hotel we saw, a place which under normal conditions would not have passed my expectations for an overnight stay. And Bako was right, it was a bright morning and we re-joined the main road east travelling through stretches of dense forest and plantations of various kinds. Traffic on the road was light and after about two hours we reached the banks of the River Niger. We crossed over the impressive iron bridge into the township of Onitsha and took the well-signposted road to my final destination, Enugu.

I had expected to enter a busy township and see roads lined with colourful market stalls and lanes choked with traffic but instead a subdued atmosphere seemed to hang over the whole place. When we reached our hotel, one of the tallest buildings in Enugu, the receptionist was clearly in a state of great anxiety. Whilst we entered our personal details into the arrivals register he told us that on the previous day the town had suffered an air raid by two planes resulting in widespread destruction and also fatalities in the industrial sector of Enugu. When I told him that I had come to visit the large spinning mill he looked at me with weepy eyes and explained that the mill and neighbouring industrial enterprises had been completely destroyed. The mill manager, a personal friend of his, had survived the raid but two young girls and a man had been killed. "I can ask him to come to the hotel," he added, "in case you want to talk to him." I readily agreed. The mill manager was still very shaken by the event and asked me that on my return to England I should contact the Sassoon Investment Bank in London, the owners of this mill, to inform them personally about the happenings here. At the moment, the mill was still a smouldering heap of rubble but tomorrow he would try to take photographs to send to London with his own full report.

I could tell from Bako's own pleading eyes that he was getting increasingly nervous about the whole situation.

After leaving Enugu, we had just reached a stretch of road flanked by large trees when we saw a single aircraft heading for Enugu. We could still see the town and specially the hotel we had just left, but we were both speechless about what happened next. A plume of smoke suddenly rose from the roof of the hotel whilst the aircraft did a wide loop over Enugu and headed west again. Bako, now looking more frightened than ever, told me with a quivering voice that the perpetrators must have been a government plane and that this was now a clear sign that the government was stepping up its action against tribal dissidents. "It could well be," he said, "that the hotel had been used by high-ranking Igbo dissidents. I already had my suspicions," he added, "because when we arrived at the hotel I saw four young men sitting in a small room near the reception area with rifles by their side. It is possible that even the leader of the dissident movement, Col. Ojukwu, was present in the building and that he was the target of this unexpected air raid." We watched the rising smoke for a little longer but Bako was anxious that we proceed with our journey.

With one spectacle behind us another one was building up in front of us. Large black clouds appeared ahead, indicating a downpour similar to what we had experienced only two days ago in Benin City. And so it was. Ten or so minutes later the skies opened up again and a torrent of water made the driving virtually impossible. Bako slowed down to a crawl but on a slight bend of the road he hit a large tree. None of us suffered any physical injuries but according to the noise at the moment of impact, the car did not do so well. We sat there shocked and dazed with Bako begging me to forgive him for his incompetence. When the rain eased off a little, he ventured outside to inspect the damage. "I have bad news," he reported, "the left front wheel is askew probably due to a twisted or broken axle." Was this the end of our motorised journey?

Fate can play many tricks on people, and we were about to become the beneficiaries of such tricks.

With the rain stopping as quickly as it had started, we saw a row of huts and houses close to the road and we saw people emerge from these buildings, rushing towards us, obviously keen to find out what had happened virtually on their doorstep. The small settlement consisted mainly of farmers and their families who did not understand English. Bako, possibly through fear of exposing himself as a Yoruba, kept silent all the time. Suddenly a middle-aged gentleman smartly dressed in jacket and trousers addressed me in fluent English and asked me to accompany him to his house. "I am a cloth and haberdashery merchant. I take it," he said, "that you are unable now to proceed with your own car. I presume that you were on your way back to Lagos." "Absolutely right," I responded. Pointing through the window he said, "Over there in that wooden hut I have a Peugeot car similar to yours. Unfortunately I have to expect that my car will be confiscated any day now by our ruling local administration. I have a cousin in Lagos who owns a small construction business and I would be pleased if you could take my car and deliver it to him when you have completed your journey."

Until about 20 minutes ago this person and I had not even known of each other and yet here he was entrusting me with what was probably his most precious possession. I expressed my heartfelt thanks and promised him that I would carry out his wish. I added that the broken-down car on the road is an ICI-owned company vehicle covered by an insurance policy. After giving me the details of his cousin in Lagos and the registration documents for his vehicle he summoned a young man to help Bako with the transfer of our baggage into his Peugeot and, surrounded by a cheering crowd, we set off for nearby Onitsha. Although Bako was keen to journey on until we reached the western side of the Niger, I decided that after such a turbulent day we should stay in Onitsha and proceed early the next morning. We found a hotel near the large bridge and concluded the day with a short stroll through this colourful township. We already noticed the high number of carts and trucks filled with a variety of household items and furniture and also livestock passing through the town heading towards the east. Little did we know that this was merely a foretaste of what we were to encounter the following morning. The hotel was very basic but clean and the bed was comfortable. As I lay in my bed thinking about the ups and downs of the past 24 hours, I noticed a lot of movement on my bedroom ceiling. A dozen or so small lizards were clinging to the ceiling performing quick movements from time to time to catch some prey, presumably mosquitoes, as we were so close to the river.

Our intention was to leave before sunrise, but Bako had to venture back into Onitsha first in search of a petrol station as the tank was nearly empty. Waiting for his return, I looked at the nearby bridge, which to my horror was teaming with people, trucks, domestic animals and vehicles of various descriptions all heading over the bridge into Onitsha. How could we possibly get through this congestion travelling in the opposite direction?

Bako, now more determined than ever to get to the other side of the river, assured me that he would find a way through this maelstrom of people and animals. "It will help," he added, "if you make yourself as visible as possible in the car as in the present situation a Western foreigner might invite less hostility than a local person." And so, with me sitting as upright as possible, Bako drove slowly into this flood of people and accompanied by a lot of shouting and angry gestures we finally reached the western side of the bridge. Although less congested than the bridge, the road was still full of people and their belongings affirming once again that this migration must have been triggered by some violent persecution and inter-tribal rivalries.

Our next stop was a settlement called Asaba, home to another large spinning and weaving mill and according to my records already a user of ICI dyestuff and chemicals. When presenting my own visiting card, I was taken straight away to meet the managing director, a gentleman of Indian descent. He appeared very upset when I told him that prior to coming to see him we had been to Enugu only to find out that the local mill had been destroyed in an air raid the day before our arrival and three workers had been killed. Thankfully the manager had escaped unharmed and I had the chance of speaking to him before leaving Enugu. "I am so glad to hear this," the managing director sighed, "because he is an old friend of mine from way back in India despite now also being my business competitor. As far as our own production is concerned, we have considered the introduction of blended yarn but the current uncertainties, now only reaffirmed by your own report of the tragic events in Enugu, has held us back from installing the necessary equipment. From all I can see at present," he said, "things will get worse before stability returns to this country." On this sombre note and with the promise that ICI will remain the favoured supplier in the future, we left for our onward journey to Lagos.

We must have been on the road for about one hour and I had dozed off when suddenly the car came to an abrupt halt. In front of us the road was blocked by three uniformed soldiers pointing their riffles at our car. One of them came forward shouting "out out!" probably the only English word he knew. We duly stepped outside the car when a more smartly dressed soldier, presumably their leader, appeared from the undergrowth at the roadside and in a kind of pidgin English demanded to see our papers and to open the boot of our car. Bako, standing next to me whispered to me, "These are Hausa soldiers" which only left me more bewildered because I had no idea how they fitted into this rapidly unfolding drama of tribal rivalries. I tried to explain to the leader that I was a businessman and on my way to Lagos but he simply commandeered two of his men to rummage through our suitcases in search of whatever. In addition to the suitcases there was also my first aid box, regularly issued to ICI employees who had to travel to tropical countries, containing plasters, bandages, antiseptic creams, water purification tablets and pills of various descriptions. When the leader opened the box himself he looked at me with a smile on his face and said, "You doctor, you must help." With that he grabbed my arm and together with my first aid box I was led a few metres through the undergrowth, suddenly facing two soldiers sitting on the ground. One of them had a badly lacerated hand and they had tried to stop the bleeding by wrapping the hand in a plant leaf. The other soldier looked miserable and clearly in some form of pain, mumbling in a strange language and pointing to his stomach. The lacerated hand was easily bandaged up but what to do with the other fellow? Was it appendicitis or simply an upset stomach or diarrhoea? Hoping for the latter two, I made him swallow two painkiller tablets and for good measure also an anti-diarrhoea pill. With proper communications being impossible, I gestured to the leader that I now wanted to return to my car and after handing over a spare fresh bandage and a tube of the antiseptic cream I was escorted back to the road. Bako, still not saying anything, had meanwhile repacked our suitcases and when he saw me jumped into the car to start the engine. The road ahead was clear but in the side mirror I could see the leader and his troupe lined up behind us still looking quite menacing with their rifles still pointing at our car. Bako, now with a smile on his face, put extra pressure on the accelerator and with a bend in the road we quickly lost sight of the Hausas.

It begs the question what would have happened if you had not been able to perform your amateurish medical service thanks to your ICI first aid box.

We shall never know the answer to that, Joseph, and at the time I was just happy to have escaped from what initially looked like a dangerous situation, not only for myself but also for Bako. Thankfully we did not encounter any further interruption on our journey. We stopped in a small village just outside Benin City for more petrol and a meal and noted to our relief that everything seemed to function in a normal and peaceful way unlike what we had just left behind us. Once again passing the almost endless plantations of palm oil trees we were now in the final phase of our eventful odyssey, and we soon reached the sprawling outskirts of Lagos. The office manager admitted that the latest reports about the rapidly escalating tensions with the eastern region had left him worried about our safety and when told that we had returned in a 'loaned' car and that the broken-down company car was left behind somewhere near Onitsha he merely congratulated us on our good fortune. I also added a glowing report on the service provided by Bako which no doubt will have raised his standing in the ICI office. Finally I was offered the facility of sending a telex message to my own office in Harrogate including a request to inform Elaine of my well-being.

Bako's final service was to drive me to the airport to catch the midday flight to Accra. It was a short flight of around one hour but after reading the headlines in the newspaper I had bought at Lagos airport I was beginning to wonder whether I should have embarked on this trip at all. Just having left a country plagued with unrest and tribal tensions it looked as if my new destination suffers from similar problems. According to the newspaper, a coup attempt had just been averted and two senior members of the military junta had been executed only two days ago.

Before setting off on my trip to West Africa, I remember, Ghana was added to my itinerary because the country, having been the first to gain its independence from British colonial rule in Africa, was widely regarded as a thriving model economy with ambitious plans for industrialisation, a policy forcefully driven forward by their initial and visionary leader Mr Nkrumah. The textile industry, with its large potential for job creation, played a leading role in Mr Nkrumah's vision for a modern Ghana. Within a short time, large investments were made in a number of spinning mills and integrated textile enterprises but after the ousting of Mr Nkrumah, Ghana's modernisation plans became the victims of political infighting and military coups and as I was about to find out few of these newly created enterprises had survived in such a volatile political and economically unstable environment.

Kotoka Airport looked a very modern airport and my passage through the control points was swift and uncomplicated. In the baggage hall I happened to stand next to a well-dressed black gentleman, who suddenly turned to me and in a kind of welcoming manner asked me, "What has brought you to visit our country?" I told him that I worked for a UK company called ICI upon which he informed me that he was a frequent visitor to London and was familiar with the role my company played in the British economy. "In fact," he added, "I have visited your impressive headquarter building near the Houses of

Parliament." Now curiosity got the better of me and I asked him what line of business he was involved in. "I work for the Ghana Cocoa Marketing Board," he replied, "and I visit your country quite regularly. It is one of our most important customers in Europe."

By the time our suitcases arrived in the baggage hall the Ghanaian Cocoa executive and I had developed quite a friendly rapport. We exchanged business cards with each other and to my surprise he added, " I have got a car waiting for me outside, I can give you a lift to the city." When I told him that I had not pre-booked any hotel accommodation he mentioned a few names in the city centre which he stressed were reasonably priced and unlikely to be overbooked at this time of year. Good fortune was obviously on my side once again.

In the arrival hall, a uniformed young man headed quickly towards us, grabbed my co-traveller's suitcase and led us outside to a highly polished Mercedes car.

During our ride to the city, I explained the purpose of my visit to Ghana. "I am afraid," my newly acquired friend replied, "that the textile sector has suffered from a severe decline and that the country instead of becoming an exporter of textiles once again relies heavily on imports. The country has slid back into the pre-Nkrumah days and my organisation is now one of the main supporters of the economy. One of the remaining large textile firms is the Ghana Textile Manufacturing Company in Tema not far from Accra. I suggest you pay them a visit as they will be better qualified to give you a more comprehensive picture of the present state of the textile industry in our country."

Our car had by now reached the busy city centre. The cocoa executive suddenly gave instructions to the driver in a local language and then turning to me he informed me that we were about to arrive at a hotel of good reputation and which was also in walking distance of Accra's famous Makola Market. "If you want to learn more of our country," he added, "then do not miss a visit to this market."

The hotel did indeed turn out to be a very welcoming place and not too expensive. With the sweltering heat outside, the air-conditioned room was a real extra bonus. The receptionist provided me with a street map of Accra and I was pleased to see that it was really only a few minutes' walk to the famous market. As I got closer to it, I could already hear loud music and ever-increasing numbers of people heading towards it. On my earlier trip to East Africa and now also Nigeria I had become quite familiar with the remarkable skill of girls and women for balancing sometimes quite large and heavy loads on their heads. The Ghanaian females seemed to be even more talented in this respect. It was quite an experience just watching them, colourfully dressed, drifting by with a basket full of vegetables or other chattels on their heads. The market itself was like the epicentre of a human eruption. Rows and rows of stalls with fruit and vegetables, artefacts, flowers, printed fabrics, crockery and many other forms of merchandise. The constant noise of shoppers haggling with stall holders or the shouting of drivers of carts trying to weave their way through the crowds gave this place an extra feeling of vibrancy. Eventually I stumbled across a refreshment stall for a much-needed drink and just sitting back enjoying the sight of shoppers passing by, many of whom with their purchases balanced delicately on their heads.

The following morning I telephoned the Ghana Textile Manufacturing Company in Tema and was very pleased that my call was immediately transferred to the general manager who not only agreed to see me but also invited me to stay for lunch. What a wonderful gesture to a person he had never met before. Judging by his voice and his perfect English during our telephone conversation, I guessed that he was an Englishman, probably someone who like Kevin in Nairobi had served in the previous colonial administration and had decided to stay on after independence. And that was indeed the case.

Before visiting the spinning mill, the general manager, who turned out to be a down-to-earth Yorkshireman, gave me what he described as a realistic picture on the present state of the textile industry in Ghana. Unfortunately it merely confirmed the views already expressed by my friendly cocoa executive. Imports from India and Korea had led to the closure of many local producers of yarns and fabrics and we ourselves, he added, had to downsize to survive. "We only make viscose and cotton yarns these days as blends with imported polyester would make us uncompetitive with the few remaining local weaving and finishing mills." Overall a rather gloomy picture. During a brief visit to his own mill the gravity of what I had just been told was demonstrated by two banks of spinning heads lying completely idle.

With Nigeria going through political turmoil and the Ghanaian textile industry in serious decline, West Africa was clearly not a region at present to provide the level of commercial opportunities we were seeking. At least we now had a clearer picture, and we could divert our efforts to more rewarding markets.

Despite all the gloom, the general manager treated me to a most enjoyable lunch at a seaside restaurant overlooking a wide stretch of a sandy beach. "No doubt," my host said, "you will know from your history classes that this shoreline was once a major departure point for slaves for the cotton and sugar plantations in the New World." I admitted that I had read several books about this sad episode in the history of mankind, adding that my own folks in Germany too are now featuring in the annals of history for the atrocities they had allowed to happen prior and during the last war. My host did not respond but I could see he understood what I was referring to.

After our lunch, my host generously offered to drive me back to my hotel in Accra and although from a business point of view I had to leave empty-handed I shall always have fond memories of this delightful country.

The next morning I caught the first available flight back to Lagos. Groups of armed soldiers swarmed round the bus taking us to the airport building and even inside an armed guard was standing outside the entrance to the transit lounge. There was quite an eerie feeling about the whole place and I felt relieved when the flight to London was called.

With a comfortable window seat, charming air hostesses offering refreshments and delicious meals and also plenty of time to cast my mind back to some of the hazardous moments during my travel in Nigeria, the whole flight was a most welcome anti-climax. I even managed to write my visit report ready for the typing pool back in the Harrogate office.

It was the 16th of May. After a slightly longer absence than originally planned I was prepared for a slightly frosty welcome and was therefore delighted when both Elaine and the dog gave me an enthusiastic 'welcome home' reception. What had happened during my absence? Was Elaine about to tell me that an addition to the family was on the way? Had she won the lottery? The answer lay spread out on the dinner table. During my absence Elaine's mother had paid a brief visit during which they must both have concluded that the time had come to move into a more prestigious and larger accommodation. The glossy brochure depicted a very attractive house built in random Yorkshire stone. It was a new development on the outskirts of Harrogate and with an initial deposit a site could be secured with the completion of the house scheduled for early spring 1968. The fact that the location was in walking distance of the office was an additional attraction. I had no hesitation in giving the project my instant approval, indeed I congratulated Elaine on having taken the initiative on such an exciting new venture.

A New Identity

Prior to my departure for West Africa, Mr Harris had mentioned the invitation he had received to visit the State Trading Organisation Exportljon in Moscow towards the end of May and that I was expected to accompany him on this trip. I was more than pleased when I now learnt that a team from Exportljon, headed by their general manager Mr Dovnja, would instead come to the UK and that business discussion could be held at the Russian Trade Mission in Highgate in London. I was delighted by these news as it would allow me to be at home for Elaine's 28th birthday.

It came as no real surprise when on the 20th of May the news reported the declaration of an independent State of Biafra by their leader Mr Ojukwu. I had just got out in time.

On the following Wednesday, the Russian Trade mission informed us that the delegation from Moscow had arrived and that a meeting with us had been marked down for the following day at 10 am. Mr Harris was convinced that a major deal with the Russians was in the making and he asked his secretary to make a luncheon booking with a lavish table setting for eight people at the Savoy Hotel on The Strand. And my export director's hunch became true. Mr Dovnja turned out to be a very amiable character. He argued tenaciously for favourable contract terms but at the same time he had the common sense to compromise when presented with sensible counter proposals. The end result was indeed a sizeable contract and it was now that Mr Harris made the invitation for the luncheon at the Savoy Hotel. Would they be able or be allowed to accept? The junior members of the Russian negotiating team cast questioning glances at each other but Mr Dovnja, without any hesitation, accepted immediately. Ending up with a group of seven people, the Russian Trade Mission offered us two chauffeured cars to drive us to the hotel.

Mr Dovnja, a portly person in his mid-fifties, turned out to be a very enjoyable table companion and not adverse to the trappings of what he jokingly referred to as the decadent Western World of Capitalism. Although he was accompanied by the official interpreter, he did not use him very much as he himself had a good command of the English language but with the underlying harshness of his own language. The hotel had well heeded the request for a lavish setting. We were shown to a beautifully laid out table with full view of the river. The gold-rimmed menus added to the splendour of this place. It soon became obvious that Mr Dovnja himself was a widely travelled person. After exchanging some war-time experiences with Mr Harris, he kept us entertained with stories about trips to remote parts of the Soviet Union and also to Cuba, where he met Fidel Castro. At this point I thought he might open his small briefcase and present Mr Harris with a box of Cuban cigars but it did not happen. He suggested however that our next meeting should be in Moscow to allow him to show off Russian hospitality. Thus was set the scene for numerous visits in the years to come.

After a two-hour lunch, crowned off with a variety of cognacs and ports, the Russians left in two taxis and Mr Harris and myself headed for Heathrow Airport to catch the early evening flight back up to Yeadon Airport.

During my short absence in London, life in Harrogate had not come to a standstill. Firstly Elaine's mother had arrived to celebrate Elaine's 28th birthday with us and to find out if we had made any progress on 'upgrading' our housing. We had to admit that nothing concrete had been done yet due to pressure at work. With her no nonsense attitude to business she suggested that we should now see the property development company and arrange a site visit to select a plot of land, if still available, and decide also on the type of house we had seen in the brochure. To give the whole matter an extra degree of urgency she added that this should all be done before she travelled back to Scotland. And so it happened. We were taken to Pannal Village to a road called Rosedale. Excavation work had already started on a few plots of land but on the left-hand side of the road we were shown an available plot with a small stream bordering one side of the property. We expressed our interest in this plot and on our return to the property company's offices in Harrogate, we agreed the total price, initial down payments and noted also some personal wishes in the internal lay-out of the house, and we signed the final contract there and then. An exciting new episode in our life had opened up. I had already derived much joy from Elaine and myself becoming the owners of our ready-built Wimpy house in Knaresborough but to see our next new home arising from scratch filled me with extra excitement.

From the way you describe your current life one can sense that you have now really settled into your adopted homeland although I suspect you must feel disappointed that once again the UK had been denied access to the great conciliatory continental project of the Common Market, which I seem to remember you were involved in during your student days and which was very close to your heart.

It is strange, Joseph, that you should bring up this matter at this stage because I was about to relate to you an incident which touches upon the hidden problems of choosing to live in a foreign land. A letter had arrived in the Harrogate office enquiring if I could be released for a senior management position in ICI's office in Frankfurt. Having unsuccessfully tried for years to persuade Elaine to make our future home in Germany, I was going to declare my disinterest in the offer even if the Harrogate office was willing to let me go. The decision to reject this prospect of promotion was made easier still when I saw the details of the terms offered. It was to be a permanent transfer and being the holder of a German passport, it would be classed as a repatriation thus excluding me from the substantial financial benefits normally granted to a UK passport holder on temporary overseas secondment. I also gained the impression that several senior colleagues in Harrogate welcomed my final rejection, and the Frankfurt office was informed accordingly. I was pleased to see that this had no adverse effect on my hitherto good relationship with the Frankfurt office.

This incidence however prompted me to start immediately the application process for my naturalisation and it took until April 1968 when I finally became the owner of a blue UK passport whilst still retaining my green West German one. My new status as a dual nationality person however did not last for long. At mid-year my West German passport became due for renewal and I submitted it and the necessary application papers to the German Consulate in Liverpool. Two weeks later I received a recorded envelope expecting it to contain my new West German passport. Instead I found my old passport with the whole top-right corner cut off plus a letter, criticising me for not having informed them about my recently acquired UK citizenship and completing the missive by informing me that in any case West Germany does not allow the status of dual nationality. That is how I became a fully-fledged UK citizen.

For the rest of the year, travelling continued at a more moderate pace and shorter durations except for the autumn trade fair in Leipzig, where I was again joined by my Greek friend Mike Miliangos. I also managed to secure my private lodgings again with the same welcoming family as the year before.

Although my visa restricted me to visiting the Leipzig Fair only, I decided one day to ignore this restriction and boarded a train to Zwickau, my mother's place of birth, to pay a surprise visit to our only remaining DDR family member, my aunt Trudel. It was quite an emotional reunion. Whilst I knew her from correspondence and photos exchanged with my mother, our last physical encounter was way back in pre-war years when I was still a toddler and we had made a family visit to Zwickau to meet not only aunt Trudel and her husband Kurt but also my maternal grandmother.

It was very hard to say goodbye, so much to say, but I had to catch the train back to Leipzig hoping that once again I would avoid any police checking travel documents.

Once again, the Trade Fair produced a good level of new and repeat business and also numerous new contacts to assist me in the still popular field of barter transactions. On my last day whilst walking through one of the halls I heard my name called out and there he was, my friendly fur dealer from New York with whom I had done my first barter deal the year before. He asked me to join him for lunch in a nearby restaurant where he told me that during this fair he had not been able to make any significant purchases but that in any case he had been looking out for me as he wanted to give me a small parcel as a thank you for last year's deal. With that, he handed me something wrapped in simple brown paper adding that he hoped it would be the right fit for my wife. "Do you remember the mink pelts I bought from the Romanians last year?" he said. "This is a small token from our own studio workshop in New York."

And there it was, a beautiful brown silk-lined mink cape. I expressed my sincere thanks, adding that he had solved the problem of a Christmas present for my wife. We parted, both hoping that we could meet up again next year.

With two more trips to Spain and Greece I concluded my travelling for 1967. Elaine and I derived great pleasure from our occasional visits to Pannal to watch the progress of the building of our new house. Our social circle kept on growing and the traditional open air shows in the surrounding villages provided refreshing entertainment with Elaine, herself turning into an accomplished flower arranger with various medals to her credit.

The Christmas and New Year break turned into another event of hectic socialising with members of the wider family and friends, so very different from the intimate and private atmosphere in which my own family had always celebrated this annual festivity in Germany.

In June 1968 we finally said goodbye to our home in Knaresborough and moved into our newly built residence in Pannal. Whenever possible I tried to reduce my amount of travelling to devote more time to helping Elaine turning our new home and the surrounding open spaces into the kind of place we could confidently show off to friends and family.

We very quickly became part of the local community and also of the small but most welcoming congregation of the Pannal village church. In fact, the local vicar and his wife turned out to be the pillars of this community and we enjoyed a close friendship with them in the years to come.

Overseas visits, although now a little less frequent, continued on a regular basis. Mr Dovnja's invitation for the next negotiation to take place in Moscow and to get a taste of Russian hospitality led to a joint visit to Moscow with my export director Mr Harris in June. The negotiation over a new contract were preceded by a succession of toasts to friendship between Britain and the USSR, the victory after the last war and the glorious revolution and other events in the calendar of Russian history. Each toast was a small beaker of vodka to be drowned in one gulp. Thankfully, prior to the contract negotiations we had been entertained in a nearby restaurant to a delicious lunch of roast pork and a variety of vegetables and the traditional borscht soup, so when it came to the procedural downing of all these vodkas, the intoxicating effect of these drinks had not seriously reduced our negotiating capacity. In fact, Mr Harris appeared to be completely unaffected whereas I, after the first three vodkas, had to admit that my capacity for quick mental arithmetic had suffered a little.

We secured a sizeable contract and spent the rest of the day sightseeing including a visit to the Hard Currency Shop in the Rossiya Hotel where I made my first ever purchase of caviar. I bought two medium-sized jars. Mr Harris decided to pay a visit to Lenin's Tomb whilst I found it more interesting to have a look round the huge GUM store. Maybe I should have gone also to visit the Lenin Tomb because the whole atmosphere and quality and display of merchandise in GUM was so disappointing that I felt like being back in East Germany in the first few post-war years.

Our taxi ride back to the hotel took us past a large pseudo-baroque-style building standing on top of a rather sinister looking black stone basement. Our driver, anxious to show off his command of English, informed us that this was the infamous Lubyanka building which had a long history of being the headquarters of different Russian secret service organisations.

Our hotel was quite close to this 'feared' building and

even there one could not completely shed the feeling of being watched and controlled, not by secret agents in dark suits and trilby hats but by rather forbidding looking female floor controllers who, sitting behind a small desk, were stationed on each hotel floor at the lift entrance/exit and demanded to see the door key of each arriving visitor.

The following morning, we were booked on an early flight back to London. Our check-in at Sheremetyevo Airport seemed to proceed quite smoothly until we came to the passport control. Having had an unhindered passage on our arrival we expected no problems on our departure. Mr Harris's passport was given only a cursory glance and he was waved on to proceed to the waiting lounge but my newly acquired British passport was examined at great length and also handed to another officer standing nearby. My thoughts flashed back to that day when I saw my then West German passport disappear through a slot in the wall of the transit room when trying to cross the East-West Border Crossing point at Helmstedt for my first visit to East Berlin. Now, with a British passport and a valid Russian visa, I had expected a trouble-free journey. But then, my birthplace Rostock was displayed also in my new passport and it must have caught the officer's attention. After a brief verbal exchange with the senior officer the controller, rather grim-faced, handed me back my passport and I was allowed to join Mr Harris again. I was quite relieved when our flight was called and I was again in the comfortable surrounds of a British aeroplane.

The rest of the year was spent with several more visits to 'behind the Iron Curtain' countries with one unexpected exception. The Singapore Broadcasting Company had expressed interest in using our polyester cables for the support of several new aerial masts on their island and our local representative felt that in this specialist sector he needed help from Head Office. After my previous involvement in a similar project in Hungary, it was agreed that I should make this visit as soon as possible. I have always been fascinated by this small but remarkable island state and its post-war recovery.

Laden with product samples and technical literature and assuring Elaine that it would at the most be a three-day trip, I set off for Singapore. Our local representative was a young Englishman called David whose own family had a long connection with the island dating back to the pre-war era. The passage through the modern airport building was swift and efficiently conducted by friendly officials. David made himself known with a large ICI placard. We drove straight to the Kempinski Hotel which was an oasis of luxury and elegance compared with the often drab establishments I had to use on my more regular visits to the communist countries in Europe. "Our meeting with the Broadcasting Authority is tomorrow morning," David explained, "but for the rest of today I will show you around our city." I enjoyed every minute of it, the feel of activity and enterprise, no beggars at street corners and over a meal in an elegant restaurant David gave me a thorough insight into ICI's business in Singapore. "With tomorrow being taken up with our business meeting and you being scheduled to fly back to the UK the following morning, I am afraid," David added, "that we shall have to give Raffles a miss. Their afternoon teas can hold their own with the Ritz in London. It is a good reason for you to visit us again sometime in the future."

Our meeting the following day was in fact with the construction company commissioned to build three masts for both radio and television transmissions. My own knowledge of such a specialist product was severely tested by the engineers of the construction company and we spent much time in discussing the data in the large volume of technical literature I had brought with me. They came to the conclusion that our product would certainly be superior to steel cables to combat insulation and static electricity problems but then they also voiced concern that the mantle of the polyester rope might suffer from exposure to the intense sunlight, common in this part of the world. I could not give them any assurances on this point and promised to obtain more information from our own scientists. In conclusion, they promised to carry out their own technical analysis of the project and to stay in contact with Harrogate. And so another challenging year came to its close. The agreement of the Superpowers in July to curb the spread of nuclear weapons had been widely welcomed as a sign that the worst of the Cold War tensions were coming to an end. Yet with Russian tanks churning up the streets of Prague only a month later to subdue the call for reform and more freedom the world were shown that the Soviet Union was not prepared to abandon its grip over its satellites.

The customary trip up to Scotland for the festive season was put into reverse with Elaine's mother visiting us in our new home in Pannal. Meantime our circle of friends had carried on expanding well beyond the confines of office colleagues and neighbours. I had to admit that with every passing month I felt more and more that my journey into the unknown only four years ago had exceeded my expectations although I was still very sore about having lost my German citizenship.

With an already snowy Christmas, the new year started with even heavier snowfalls. On several days, attempts to reach the office with our motorcar had to be abandoned and Elaine and I had to walk through deep snow from our

Pannal village across fields to Harrogate. Even air traffic was affected by these severe weather conditions. This gave me a welcome opportunity to spend some time in the office. After discussions with a variety of senior staff I finally drew up a plan of commercial targets for the rest of the year. This resulted in a clear priority of not only Western Europe where local offices and agencies were increasingly capable of promoting the wide spectrum of IC's business but also the state-controlled economies behind the Iron Curtain, which, despite the Cold War, were still eager to do business with the 'decadent' West.

With severe winter conditions still raging, my first visit was to Bucharest. Whilst purchases on a barter basis were still very much in vogue in Romania, I was assured that such a condition would not have to be applied to our next contract. The chief buyer was a very charming and attractive middle-aged lady by the name of Munteanu who not only spoke fluent English but conducted the whole negotiation in a most civilised manner, unlike the often very reserved and sullen behaviour of negotiating partners in other Comecon countries. Behind all her charm, however, she was hiding a sharp mindset for her business remit and she left no stone unturned for getting the best possible deal.

With the prospects of Romania becoming a significant customer for our products, I decided to also contact the British Embassy in Bucharest to introduce myself to the commercial attaché.

The wintery conditions I had left behind in the UK existed even more severely here in Bucharest. Due to heavy snowfalls the airport was closed for several hours whilst several snowploughs busily cleared the runway by pushing the snow to either side, creating walls nearly three metres high. After a three-hour delay my flight was eventually called. The aircraft gently manoeuvred itself onto the cleared runway readying itself for take-off. As the aircraft started speeding down the runway it felt like racing through a glen with walls of snow on both sides and the tips of the wings missing the snow walls only by half a metre or so. This precarious take off from Bucharest left a lasting impression on me.

The next few months were filled with visits to Hungary, Bulgaria and Poland. My travelling however came to a sudden halt when Elaine had an unexpected gall bladder infection and had to be admitted to a Harrogate Hospital. It was the first time I had seen Elaine so incapacitated, but her lady doctor assured me that she would soon be on her feet again. Her mother rushed down from Scotland to be by her side and to make sure that our dog was well looked after.

I am surprised that your vivid and detailed recollections rarely include any comments on social, political and scientific events both locally and also in the countries you visit.

I can assure you, Joseph, that being an almost fanatical reader of newspapers and follower of televised news I have always considered myself well informed about happenings around the globe. In fact my obsession with news often invited scolding comments from Elaine. However, when making the UK my new home country I decided from the outset not to express any personal views on political issues or join a political party, a decision which also guided me in my dealings with my trading partners behind the Iron Curtain.

My chosen political impartiality however was not shared by my wife. After returning from a visit to Prague I found to my amazement that Elaine had offered our garage to the Conservative Party as a campaign centre for local elections. Since we were both joint owners of our house,

I had to accept that her action was well within her rights. In any case, Elaine's brief participation in the UK political arena was soon overshadowed by the phenomenal news of mankind's first landing on the moon.

The rest of the year was filled with visits to ICI offices and agencies in both Western and Eastern Europe and also attending functions at London-based embassies of the Iron Curtain countries. At the annual Leipzig autumn fair I had the opportunity to meet up again with my old mentor Mike Miliangos whose business was clearly flourishing as he told me that apart from his villa in Hamburg he now also owned an apartment in Montreux to be near his Crimplene producing factory. When I told him that Elaine and I had planned a late holiday to Germany he hoped that we could spare a couple of days to be his guests in Switzerland.

Looking at the results of my activities in Western and Eastern Europe, the export director Mr Harris decided that repeat visits to Africa should be put on hold as the follow-up business after my visits to both East and West Africa did not meet the original expectations. Also Mr Harris indicated that he himself would like to accompany me on the occasional visit to Eastern Europe. Maybe our joint trip to Exportljon in Moscow and two visits to the Soviet Trademission in Highgate in London had given him a taste for dealing with people from that part of the world. When I mentioned that I had planned a visit to Bucharest for early in the new year he expressed interest in travelling with me.

It must have been March when this visit finally took place. With company directors being normally booked into more upmarket hotels, the Harrogate travel office had made a booking at one of Bucharest's best known hotels, the Athenae Palace. As we soon discovered it was not only the hotel chosen by other, mainly Western visitors, but also a place which attracted a host of young good-looking and well-dressed ladies who did their utmost in attracting the attention of male visitors. Whilst Mr Harris and I had a drink at the bar, two of these ladies joined us and, speaking in almost fluent English, they pretended to be members of the Bucharest Ballet. After half an hour of lighthearted conversation in the course of which our two 'companions' asked many questions about our personal and professional background and the purpose of our visit to Bucharest, one of them suddenly pulled a camera from her handbag and suggested she took a picture of both Mr Harris and myself. Before I could even voice my objection, the flash on the camera went off and our picture had been taken.

After the two mystery ladies had left us, I explained to Mr Harris that they were most likely members of the Romanian State Security Service and that our faces were now in their records. Little did we know at this stage that we would be the target of further encounters with these two self-confessed ballet dancers.

The following day I visited the State Trading Organisation Romanoexport to negotiate a new order for our polyester tow product. Mrs Munteanu greeted me like an old friend which did not stop her from negotiating very tenaciously over the new contract.

Mr Harris had decided to visit the UK Embassy to learn more about the wider commercial relationship between the UK and Romania and to introduce himself as a representative of the UK's largest industrial enterprise.

The following morning, during our taxi ride to the airport, Mr Harris asked me if I had had any disturbance the previous night. I had intended not to mention the late knock on my door when one of the two 'ballet dancers' had turned up to offer me her company for the night but after telling him about this attempted intrusion, Mr Harris explained that he also had had a late night visit from one of the two 'ballet dancers', in fact the one who had photographed us before, making also an offer of nocturnal companionship.

Having already come to the conclusion after our first encounter that these two young ladies were most likely members of the State Secret Service it now appeared that part of their remit included the more intimate activity of being honeytraps. Mr Harris, as I now learnt, had equally expressed his annoyance with this late-night intrusion by quickly slamming the door in the visitor's face.

On our flight back to the UK we talked more about this unexpected incidence and when I stressed the good commercial relationship I enjoyed with Romanoexport and the sizeable contract just obtained, we could not think of any reason why we should have become targets of scrutiny by the local secret service. Maybe, Mr. Harris concluded, these two 'ballet dancers' were in fact just professional gold diggers, targeting well-to-do foreign visitors in this upmarket hotel. This may well have been the right conclusion because during my future regular visits to Romania, on one occasion even accompanied by Elaine, and my ongoing good relationship with Romanoexport, there were no signs of being subjected to any form of surveyance. In fact I always looked forward to visiting Bucharest. On one of these visits I even had the 'honour' of meeting the rather overbearing Mrs Ceausescu at an official Trade reception organised by the UK Embassy.

With a late holiday in Freiburg, including a two-day trip to Montreux as guests of Mr Miliangos, another eventful year was coming to a close.

I had hoped that the demands for travelling in 1970 would be less severe but it was not to be the case. My Vienna-based assistant Reinhold Bethusy, who had made regular visits to the State Trading Organisations in Czechoslovakia and Hungary, was called back to our Harrogate Offices for other duties, leaving me with increased travelling to these two important markets for our products. In the past, I had always enjoyed the occasional joint visit with Reinhold as it enabled me to route my return to the UK via Vienna where Reinhold, with his profound knowledge of the city, could indulge me in the culinary and cultural pleasures of this beautiful locality.

Although I would have loved another trip to the Far East, my manager felt that Western and Eastern Europe required my main attention. The expiry of ICI's polyester patent had led to a sudden loss of the fees so far received from European and also Japanese licence holders and the battle for market share by all producers had intensified. This increased competition became particularly apparent in the state-controlled economies of Eastern Europe. Consequently, my visits to all the Comecon capitals became almost a matter of routine, in addition to attending the Leipzig Trade Fair, attending embassy receptions and visiting our Harrogate staff seconded to several ICI Offices in Western Europe. On one of my visits to ICI's Frankfurt Office I also had the opportunity to make a long overdue visit to my mother in Freiburg who had settled down in a more modern apartment in the Loretto Strasse.

At home, Elaine bore my frequent absence with admirable fortitude. She was well looked after by an ever-growing circle of friends and colleagues. Also the occasional weekend trip to Scotland helped to keep the marriage on an even keel. In all our relationships, I always had the feeling that the courtesy and friendliness extended to Elaine could also be shared by me. This belief however was severely shattered when one night, whilst sound asleep, a large brick crashed through the street-facing window of our bedroom and hit the wall just above my head. To this day I cannot think of any person who would have expressed his anger with me in such a violent fashion and I only felt sorry for Elaine having to share such a traumatic event with me. Realising that the perpetrator would not linger at the scene of his crime, I suggested we go back to sleep, ignoring Elaine's plea to telephone the police. Thankfully I never had to suffer such form of aggression again and as time passed, I even made myself believe that the perpetrator may have targeted our house by mistake. I shall never know.

During May and June, I followed with special interest the often quite bruising election campaign between the Tories and the Labour Party. Although now as a UK passport owner I was entitled to cast my vote, I continued with my originally adopted policy of neutrality but lived in hope that the British public would give Mr Heath a resounding victory because of his well-known sympathy for making the UK a member of the European family of nations. Although the victorious Mr. Heath suffered serious setbacks during his premiership, I have always held him in high esteem for overcoming the hitherto intransigent Gallic opposition and for finally reaching an agreement with the French President Mr Pompidou. It was a special celebratory day for me when in October the House of Commons approved the UK accession to the European Economic Market. Strange as it may sound but it suddenly made me feel even less of a foreigner in the UK, even with Elaine not entirely sharing my enthusiasm.

My growing feeling that the UK was moving towards joining the family of continental nations was further strengthened when in February the pound sterling was officially decimalised. I have to admit that ever since first setting foot in the UK I have battled with the profusion of measurements, be it temperatures in Fahrenheit and Celsius, distances in inches, feet, yards and miles and above all the division of the pound sterling. Although I always prided myself on a good level of mental numeracy I had until now always left it to the honesty of the shop keepers to give me the right change after a purchase.

My travels to both Western and Eastern Europe had become almost a routine. The business, particularly with the Iron Curtain economies, was growing steadily. The barter trading had virtually ceased and the social and cultural scene had greatly improved. More and more shops in East European capitals were beginning to offer an increasing variety of good-quality traditional goods. The food in some of the pricier restaurants was reaching almost Western standards. Pre-bookings of hotel rooms could be relied upon and when it failed, as it once did in Warsaw, all efforts were made to provide me with a resting place albeit on this occasion only in a bathtub with cushions and a thick blanket.

Whilst East and West were still in a state of Cold War Europe was at least spared the horrors of bloody conflicts which were still raging through the Asian subcontinent and parts of Africa.

I get the impression you are developing a kind of love affair with Eastern Europe.

I would not go that far, Joseph, but during my many visits I certainly learnt to admire the resilience of people to government-dictated lifestyles and their clinging to Christian beliefs. Strange as it may sound, the one country which continued to give me a feeling of unease was the GDR, my own homeland. Whilst I very much enjoyed the almost cosmopolitan atmosphere of the Leipzig fair, visits to the Berlin-based State Trading Organisation always filled me with trepidation. The sight of the intimidating wall and the pointed questions when passing through Checkpoint Charlie never ceased to give me a strong feeling of discomfort even now as the holder of a UK passport

My annual visiting programme continued to include also the commercial attachés at the London-based embassies of these East European countries. It was on 28th August when I visited also the Soviet Trade Delegation Offices in Highgate to discuss a repeat contract for the autumn. The official in charge was a Mr Lyalin whom I had met before on my joint visit with our export director Mr Harris.

Not only speaking English very fluently, Mr Lyalin had all the appearances and mannerisms of a London business executive. He told me that he was waiting for instructions from Exportljon in Moscow to find out if another visit had to be made to Moscow or if he could conclude a deal here in London. It all sounded very promising which prompted me to invite him for lunch at Fortnum & Mason. He readily accepted and ordered a car from the delegation's own fleet to drive us there. After a very convivial lunch, we parted company and I caught the train back to Harrogate for the weekend break. It must have been the following Tuesday when I read in my morning paper that a Mr Oleg Lyalin, professing to be a member of the feared Soviet State Security Organisation, the KGB, had been arrested in London on a drink/drive charge. What appeared to be a minor misdemeanour by a Russian national however turned into a serious diplomatic rift between the USSR and the UK. I had noticed before that Mr Lyalin had expressed sympathetic views about the Western lifestyle but now he had decided not only to break ranks with his previous employer but had agreed to disclose the names of a large number of other KGB members working as spies under the umbrella of the Russian Embassy and other establishments in the UK. It was only a few weeks later that 105 Russians were expelled from the UK. As to be expected, Moscow retaliated speedily by expelling 18 members of the UK Embassy.

Where did all this leave me? I was probably the last recorded person with whom Mr Lyalin had held official business discussions at the Trade Delegation Offices. Will my name now appear in KGB files and expose me to questioning or even detention on future visits to Moscow?

I shared my concern with my manager and also Mr Harris and it was agreed that we should wait to see who would take over the role of Mr Lyalin at the Trade Delegation Office. In the meantime, we should continue to maintain our contact with the Moscow-based State Trading Organisation Exportljon by fax and correspondence. This did indeed lead to a sizeable contract in November which seemed to indicate that the diplomatic rift had not affected our good commercial relationship. I felt very relieved.

On the social side, both Elaine and I felt blessed with the ever-growing circle of friends and acquaintances. We enjoyed playing host to them in our Pannal house and sharing outings with them to the large number of picturesque inns and restaurants in the countryside surrounding Harrogate. We kept particularly close with the Petrie family who had so generously adopted me when I first arrived in Harrogate in 1963. But there was also the Munroe family who, with their Scottish background, made Elaine always feel especially comfortable. The Tweedie family, who lived just round the corner from us, were not only a source of entertainment and generosity, but their occasional matrimonial disagreements required us to act as untrained marriage counsellors. Then

I must not forget the long-lasting friendship with two generations of the Carlene family with the head of the family being Dr Carlene, the senior ICI Fibres executive whose secretary happened to be Elaine.

A letter from Germany earlier in the year had informed us that my brother Lothar and his family had finally decided to leave South Africa and to return to Freiburg. Our last encounter was in 1966 during my short and ill-fated visit to Johannesburg. With Lothar's son Michael having reached schooling age and feeling also increasingly concerned about the growing racial and political tensions in the country, my brother and his wife Erika came to the conclusion to end their comfortable existence in Johannesburg and to resettle back in Freiburg.

My mother was clearly pleased that at least one of her wandering sons had returned home.

Year-end festivities centred around our own home in Pannal with Elaine's mother playing a lively role as an accomplished co-host.

1972 had all the signs of following the pattern of visits to both Western and Eastern countries with the trade fair in Leipzig being, as usual, one of the most interesting events of the year. When I was also sent for a fortnight to an ICI-owned management training centre near London, I looked upon this as a sign that some promotion might be on its way. Whilst the results of my commercial work had been well recognised in annual salary increases, my status as a TO (Technical Officer) had remained the same as when I started in 1963. For some time now I had felt that my official status should have risen to at least an assistant manager level but to my disappointment, shared also by several of my colleagues, a number of management positions were given to members of the now fully owned British Nylon Spinners Company as part of the integration process.

It must have been late November when my export director Mr Harris asked to see me. Was he interested in another joint visit to an Iron Curtain country? Had my sales figures not reached his expectation? Or was he going to tell me that at long last I had been promoted?

"We have had an enquiry from our ICI Headquarters at Millbank in London," he started, "asking us if we could nominate a suitable candidate for the role as deputy manager for the Eastern Europe Department based in Millbank, starting in mid to late January in 1973. I thought," he added, "that with your many years of dealing with the state-controlled economies, this might be a position for which you are well qualified. According to the job description they have sent us the candidate needs to acquaint himself with the activities of all the major divisions of the ICI group of companies, negotiate with the individual State Authorities, the setting up of ICI Offices, recruit local staff, organise exhibitions and assist also with the reception of senior Communist state officials on visits to ICI's London headquarters and to any of the company's UK-based manufacturing and research establishments. We would be sorry to see you go," he concluded, "but it is certainly a step up the ladder for you if we respond positively to Millbank and you pass the interview successfully."

Just listening to the job description, I thought that the demands for travelling would certainly not diminish, possibly the opposite.

As we drove back to Pannal that evening and I had given Elaine an outline of my meeting, she added to the excitement of the day by telling me she might be pregnant. How much more could happen in just one day? For the next two days we discussed the pros and cons, finally reaching the conclusion that my career progression should be the dominant factor. Elaine did not fail to point out however that a move to the London area would add another 200 miles to the journey to Elderslie.

Still with mixed feelings, particularly with Elaine's now confirmed pregnancy, I informed Mr Harris of our decision and just prior to Christmas I was informed that I should present myself for an interview in London at 3 pm hours on 8th of January.

The main theme of discussions with friends and neighbours during the festive season was the possibility of me being offered the London job and us having to relocate to a new home. We loved our beautiful Pannal house, built with random Yorkshire stone and a stream bordering our back garden. I was therefore not surprised when Elaine insisted that if we really were to move it should also be a random stone-built property. Little did she know that such properties are extremely rare in the counties around London.

Having previously spent some time in London as a management trainee of J. & P. Coats, I was quite familiar with the area around the Houses of Parliament but I had never paid any attention to ICI's massive headquarter building in Millbank. As I approached the entrance, I was quite awestruck by the enormous front door, possibly made in stainless steel, depicting in great detail the industrial activities administered and controlled from this building. Just looking at this door I could see why this giant conglomerate had the word 'Imperial' in its official company name.

Once inside, a uniformed employee took me up to the third floor to meet the head of the Overseas Department and also the manager of the East European Section, Mr Martin Wray.

The interview covered not only my past work for the ICI Fibres Division but my interviewers also seemed to be very interested in hearing more about my teenage years in East Germany and the escape to the West in 1950. Had I learnt any of the East European languages? I mentioned that I had a very limited knowledge of Russian as it had become a compulsory subject in all schools in the GDR in the post-war years. However as a form of clandestine protest for removing the previously taught Latin and ancient Greek from the curriculum plus the dismissal of our previous teachers, I and most of my fellow pupils had put little effort into learning Russian and we deliberately failed most of the exams. I did not mention the episode with Mr Lyalin the previous year as I felt that my interviewers might look upon this as a potential risk factor.

On the whole, the interview had gone quite well and, on parting, Mr Wray told me that my local management in Harrogate would be informed of the result within the next few days.

Three days later the Harrogate personnel manager appeared in my office to let me know that my interview had been successful and that I was expected in London on the 8th of February. Had I done the right thing?

I was about to ask you the same question. Firstly, a pregnant wife, an impending relocation to the London area with all the usual problems of selling your present property and finding a new suitably located home, then handing over your current responsibilities to your successor in Harrogate plus no doubt a multitude of other challenges.

Yes, Joseph, I am not surprised by your question but as so often in the past good fortune stood by my side. With Elaine's mother making sure her pregnant daughter was not left on her own, and ICI, both in Harrogate and also in London, promising generous help whenever needed, I confidently walked through those imposing front doors again on the 8th of February and was shown to my own spacious office with a view straight out onto the River Thames. It was agreed that our domestic relocation would be delayed until Elaine had given birth sometime in July and that I could spend the weekends in our Pannal home. During the week I had the use of a small apartment in a tenement building near the Buckingham Palace Gardens.

Mr Wray, with whom I established an immediate good rapport, suggested that during the first couple of weeks I visit the ICI Divisions already involved in trade with the Comecon economies and to acquaint myself with their key products and any trading problems they might have. With ICI companies spread from Scotland to Slough in Berkshire I looked forward to an interesting domestic travel programme, which allowed me to also incorporate a few extra returns to our Pannal home.

Back in London, Mr Wray used our lunch breaks to introduce me to several members of other Millbank departments. The discussions and arguments highlighted very quickly that in ICI's head office people looked at national and international issues in a more detached and critical fashion. My new colleagues often sounded like macroeconomists with sometimes opposing geopolitical opinions. I learnt a lot about the global aspirations of ICI and the wide range of its affiliates' activities. The recent admission of the UK to the European Economic Community provided additional material for lively exchanges which to my delight were mainly in favour of this historic event.

My first trip back behind the Iron Curtain was to Romania where I was hoping that my old trading partner, Romanoexport, could help me to start what I feared could be a long process of obtaining governmental permission for setting up an ICI office. They did not disappoint me. That very same afternoon I had a meeting at their Ministry for Trade and Industry where I was given the necessary application papers with the instructions to return them via the UK Embassy in Bucharest. Once returned and approved, ICI was free to seek the necessary office accommodation and start hiring personnel via a state-owned placing agency. It all looked much easier than I had expected. I paid a brief visit to the commercial attaché at the UK Embassy to keep him fully posted before heading back for London.

Feeling very encouraged by the positive reaction in Bucharest, my next target was Poland. Before setting off I contacted the Polish Embassy in London. The commercial attaché very readily provided me with details of the authority in Warsaw, responsible for international trade relations.

Deliberately or by accident, my secretary even booked my flight with the Polish State airline LOT whose fleet in those days consisted entirely of Russian-made aircraft. Having become accustomed to the comforts of BA and BOAC flights in the past, the Russian-built aircraft had a decidedly utilitarian feel about it. The welding seams of the seat frames looked rough and sometimes unfinished, the upholstery of the seats was flat and shabby looking and the overhead space for hand luggage was very small. It took some time before LOT lost its jocose description amongst my colleagues as 'LAST OVERSEAS TRIP'.

As the years went by, Poland acquired a range of modern Western aircraft and the in-flight service was of high quality.

In the past, when visiting Warsaw as a representative of ICI Fibres, I had stayed several times at the Bristol Hotel where I got to know the manager quite well. Not having pre-booked hotel accommodation on this occasion, I thought I would try the Bristol Hotel again and instructed the taxi driver accordingly. The manager happened to be in the reception area and expressed his delight at seeing me back again. "Of course," he said, "there is a room available for you." On our last encounter, I remember him insisting, that with a surname like Pietrek I must really be Polish although he knew from my passport that I was born in Germany.

A call to the telephone number given to me by the attaché in London led to an instant invitation to the Ministry for Trade and Industry. It became clear very soon that the authorities would welcome ICI strengthening their commercial activities with Poland and that the establishment of an ICI Office in Warsaw had their full support. I felt quite pleased with myself. It certainly appeared that at least the Cold War was getting a little less cold. Which unfortunately could not be said for the simmering tensions in the Middle East.

It all gave me hope that my next two target countries, Hungary and Czechoslovakia, would be equally supportive. Initial visits to their London-based embassies already provided grounds for optimism and my instant visit to these countries was only delayed by my manager asking me to coordinate first of all the participation of several major ICI Divisions at an international trade fair at Plovdiv in Bulgaria and also to attend the fair myself.

I was beginning to get quite nervous about overseas travel now with the prenatal test showing that Elaine would give birth early to mid-July. After my return from Plovdiv, I therefore decided to take my full annual leave from the end of June and return to Harrogate/Pannal. My search for a new home in the London area had so far been unsuccessful but at least I had marked out the locations which allowed a swift commuter service to my London office and very importantly were also in reasonable proximity to the two airports of Heathrow and Gatwick.

It was an established routine for the head of the Overseas Department to call a meeting every Monday morning attended by the managers of the Regional Sections. With my manager Mr Wray being unavailable on this occasion I attended on his behalf. The lead topic was the oil crisis and ICI's problem of securing supplies of naphtha, previously sourced from the Soviet Union and vitally needed in various manufacturing processes throughout the group of ICI companies. Once back in my office, I remembered that my old friend and mentor Mike Miliangos had once mentioned his involvement in the oil trade. I decided to give him a quick telephone call at his Hamburg residence and after explaining the problem to him, he indicated to my amazement that he might be able to help but would need financial help and guaranties from ICI.

When I passed the news to the head of the Department, he suggested that my friend comes as soon as possible to London at ICI's expense to hopefully reach an agreement on all terms and conditions. He finally thanked me for the action I had taken.

Two days later my friend arrived at Millbank, the negotiations were successful and only four weeks later a tanker load of Russian naphtha arrived at ICI's large Teesside complex.

It was the end of June when I finally started my annual leave, not only sharing with Elaine the crucial final days of her pregnancy but also enjoying again the company of old ICI Fibres colleagues and friends and neighbours. The great day finally arrived on 13th July when after a long labour and the need for forceps intervention, Elaine gave birth to our son Nicholas at the Harrogate General Hospital. A new chapter in our lives had begun.

With Elaine's mother rendering much appreciated

assistance and my annual leave coming to an end, I once again had to head south with the added urgent task of finding a new home for our enlarged family. I finally came to the conclusion that the county of Surrey offered the most suitable location. After visits to numerous estate agents and touring a large number of attractive villages, I finally found a property in a village called Bramley near Guildford. An attractive-looking and spacious house, it met all the conditions for a comfortable family life, in addition to which it was ideally located for my future commuting to London and in easy reach of the UK's leading airports, Heathrow and Gatwick. To crown it all, it even had an entrance porch built with random natural stone.

It must have given you a great feeling of relief and satisfaction finally having found a new home for your and your family's new life in the south.

Yes, Joseph, I sometimes felt I was dreaming all this, but the harsh reality was never far away. Thankfully it took only four weeks for our Pannal house to be sold but the proceeds left us decidedly short for the purchase of the Bramley property and only a sizeable new mortgage allowed us to finally conclude the deal. Before our final farewell in Pannal, our son Nicholas was baptised in our local Pannal church with the baptismal gathering not only including Nicholas's godmother and Elaine's longstanding friend, Helga Spring, but to our great delight also Elaine's previous boss Dr Carlene and his family.

With Elaine overseeing the refurbishment of our new home, I had to accustom myself to life as a commuter, interrupted only by quite frequent car journeys to the nearby airports.

The time had now come to make the delayed visits to Hungary and Czechoslovakia and to formalise the setting up of ICI offices.

Down to Earth

Over the years I had become quite fond of both Prague and Budapest. They both had escaped the ravages of the last war and Prague in particular, with all its architectural splendour, had a special attraction for me. It was also the place where in 1965 I had staged the ICI Crimplene fashion show. Ever since then, my business relationship with that country had flourished and I felt confident that I would have no problems in now obtaining the permission for establishing an official ICI office. In fact, during my discussion with the State Ministry, the officials suggested that a junior employee would give me a helping hand in the search for premises and later on also for office staff. Before heading off for the airport, I paid a visit to the famous Moser shop to purchase a beautiful crystal fruit bowl as a decorative addition to our own new home.

My initial reception in Budapest was more reserved. They were still waiting for the necessary laws to be passed before allowing the establishment of foreign commercial offices. During our discussion it became clear however that Hungary had a genuine desire to develop deeper relationships with the Western world. A courtesy visit to my old trading partner, Hungarotex, brought back memories of my days as the ICI Fibre representative. As another act of nostalgia, I decided to conclude the day with a meal at the famous Matyas Pince Restaurant and as ever the atmosphere and the sound of traditional music made one feel in another world.

Did you and Elaine and baby Nicholas settle in well in your new home?

Very much so, Joseph. The removal of all our belongings from Pannal was a flawless operation, the Bramley house had undergone a complete redecoration and the new neighbours gave us a welcome, more spontaneous than I had ever experienced in Yorkshire. The fact that several of our new neighbours became fellow commuters to London also helped us to become quickly part of our new local community. Attending Sunday services in the local Holy Trinity Church also helped to build up a wider circle of acquaintances in the village. Son Nicholas made good progress and gave us more undisturbed nights than we had expected. The special feature of Christmas 1973 was that my mother could also join us to greet her grandson.

Early January we received official permission for the opening of the office in Bucharest which I followed up with an immediate visit. The Ministry had a list of premises available for foreign applicants. I spent the next two days looking at a variety of apartments, some of them consisting of just one room. In the end I decided on a spacious three-room apartment above a restaurant in the centre of Bucharest not far from the Athenae Palace Hotel, the place which brought back memories of the joint visit with Mr Harris.

With a list of instructions on the settlement of rental costs, the remuneration of future local staff, I returned to London to seek Mr Wray's approval and to start informing all the various ICI Divisions of the corporate action we were taking in Iron Curtain countries.

A large part of the year was taken up with dealing with the administrative aspects of opening these new ICI offices, including the recruitment of local staff. With the East German State Trading Organisation located in the eastern part of the divided city, it was thought preferable to locate an ICI employee in the western section of Berlin.

A welcome interruption to my now almost routine programme of flying in and out of these eastern countries came when Mr. Wray asked me to assist him with the setting up of an ICI's corporate stand at the International Trade Fair in Moscow. Since my last visit as an ICI Fibres representative, I had not been back to Moscow and the prospect of seeing more of this city was appealing. But what about that interlude with Oleg Lyalin in London in 1971? In the end I decided to inform Mr Wray about my encounter with Oleg Lyalin. "I remember that case very well," he replied, "but I do not think that your purely commercial meeting with him and also the fact that during the last year you have to your knowledge not encountered any obvious scrutiny in any of the Moscow satellite states should give us any reason for concern at the forthcoming International Trade Fair. After all," he added, "the Russians are eager to attract prestigious international companies like ICI to attend their fair and it would only be to their disadvantage if they caused problems to foreign participants. Just do not plan any foreign visits until we get your passport back with the visa for the duration of the fair." It all sounded very sensible and I felt very relieved. The only remaining concern was the length of my likely absence as Elaine's second pregnancy was now becoming very visible and I felt I should not leave her unattended for too long. Mr Wray fully agreed with me and suggested that I do ICI stand duties for just three days.

I am amazed you did not mention such an important event such as Elaine's new pregnancy before.

Well, Joseph. I became reluctant to share news of such a happy event too readily ever since in our early married life Elaine had suffered a miscarriage which left her with a psychological scar until finally our son Nicholas was born.

At the end of September I applied for my visa and was pleased it was granted without any further questions. Since my last passage through Moscow's Sheremetyevo Airport, the whole place seemed to have had a more modern and welcoming refurbishment and was buzzing with visitors to the trade fair. What had not changed was the taxi driver's underhand request to be paid in dollars or pounds. The Hotel National where I had stayed before had not changed, with stern-looking female floor stewards still controlling the comings and goings of all guests.

ICI's stand at the fair was impressive. It was spacious and displayed a diversity of activities which left no one in doubt that this company was amongst Europe's leading enterprises. I even had the opportunity to welcome again staff from Exportljon, my old trading partner during my days with ICI Fibres. For two evenings, I shared my dinner with colleagues from ICI's Dyestuffs and Mond Division and unchanged from past experience the service was slow and getting the bill settled was as much a struggle as ever.

Amongst all the posters and billboards at the fair I had noticed a very striking one promoting the Moscow State Circus as a once in a lifetime experience. Our stand manager, an employee of the local Trading House Golodetz, a firm which closely collaborated with ICI, confirmed that next to going to a performance at the Bolshoi Theatre, a visit to the Circus was an absolute must. And he was right. The impressive domed building alone was a sight to behold and judging by the size of it, it would probably match the Royal Albert Hall in London. It all turned into a very memorable evening with incredible trapeze performances without safety nets, displays of superb horsemanship and a multitude of animal tamers showing their skills with fear-inspiring tigers, bears and other animals of the wild.

The next morning before catching my flight back to London, I even had a chance to visit the nearby Rossiya Hotel, a building of enormous dimensions but more importantly to me, also the home of a large Hard Currency Shop offering high-quality merchandise and delicatessen to clients fortunate enough to be able to pay in dollars or any other convertible Western currency. I stocked up with a few jars of caviar at what I thought was a very reasonable price and could not resist also buying one of those famous Russian wooden nesting dolls.

Back in Bramley, Elaine and son Nicholas continued to widen our social circle, particularly in our immediate neighbourhood which seemed to abound with young mothers and their toddlers. It looked as if my absence had not been missed very much at all. In the office, however, a message was waiting for me to revisit Bucharest to meet the staff selected by the authorities to work in the sanctioned ICI Office.

It was to be my last visit of the year. Two persons were presented to me, one a youngish looking man in his mid-thirties called Rodescu, and Ana-Maria who had just finished her university studies. Both appeared to be intelligent and well-mannered people and had a good command of the English language. We agreed the terms of employment there and then. The following day we spent in the new office premises to decide on the required office furniture and I provided them with information about the various State Trading Organisations who were already trading with ICI or who were of potential interest for the future. Regarding their own future work, I told them that delegates from our various ICI Divisions would arrive after the festive season to discuss with them in more detail the type of help and support needed in future. I also promised an early return visit in the new year. On my way back to the airport, I stopped off at the UK Embassy to inform the commercial attaché of our new office venture. He reported that there had been a noticeable increase lately in major British companies trying to strengthen their presence in Romania, with even licensing arrangements under discussion.

My plans for the new year were not only the completion of the office arrangements in Poland, Czechoslovakia and Hungary but to seek also a stronger ICI presence in Yugoslavia. This country, although ideologically linked to the Marxist masters in Moscow, tried to follow its own form of socialism and had become an important buffer zone between East and West during the Cold War years. Belgrade had become a thriving business centre and their leader Mr Tito had succeeded in welding together the numerous and often feuding Balkan regions into what appeared to have become a coherent state.

With Elaine's pregnancy progressing well and a likely birth predicted for mid-April, we decided to grant ourselves a special family treat by booking our first cruise holiday, our destination being the Norwegian fjords. It was an unforgettable experience and the forerunner for many more cruises in the years to come. Son Nicholas was the youngest passenger on the ship and was spoilt with attention from both crew members and fellow passengers.

Back in the office, news had arrived that both Poland and Czechoslovakia would allow the ICI Office to be headed by a UK citizen, leading to the search for suitable and willing candidates amongst the different ICI Divisions. Offering secondments to Warsaw or Prague did not have the same appeal as spending some time in a Western European country but in the end our first two candidates joined our East European Department in March. I had stopped my own travelling for the time being and on 11th of April I rushed Elaine to the Mount Alvernia Hospital in Guildford, where she gave birth to our son Christopher. I stayed with her during the birth and before I could take a proper look at my newborn son he was wrapped up by the Catholic nun acting as a midwife and carried away to the Hospital Chapel for a blessing. It was a glorious sunny day and Elaine had the glow of a proud mother on her face. When Christopher was returned to us from the chapel, we both shared a moment of unconstrained happiness.

It was a week later that Mr Wray told me that he would be travelling with the ICI chairman, Mr Callard, for a high-level meeting in Moscow. Little did I know at that moment what repercussions this visit would have on my own future. Regarding the events which unfolded in Moscow, I can only report here what Mr Wray told me after his sudden return to London. His revelations opened up the window on the underhand activities of spying and information gathering between the East and the West. As a fluent Russian speaker and before joining ICI in the early 60s, Mr Wray had been working for the UK counterespionage organisation MI6 where one of his colleagues was a certain Mr George Blake. Both of them spent some time together in West Berlin with the task of monitoring Russian telephone communication and, if possible, even tap underground cables from tunnels dug under the Berlin Wall. In 1961, George Blake was finally exposed as a double agent and given a very long prison sentence. His sensational escape from Wormwood Scrub in 1966 and his subsequent reappearance in Moscow made worldwide news at the time. This set the scene for what was about to happen during the visit of the chairman and Mr Wray to Moscow.

Their pre-booked accommodation was in the grand

Rossiya Hotel. With the official meeting scheduled for the following morning, both the chairman and Mr Wray decided to have an early night. At around 9 pm Mr Wray had a knock on his bedroom door and when opening it found himself face to face with his erstwhile colleague from the MI6 days, George Blake, requesting a personal talk. Without much delay, George Blake let it be known that the Russian State Security Agency, the KGB, was looking for new collaborators in the UK with good knowledge of the industrial world and that a person like Mr Wray could be a valuable collaborator. This was quickly followed by threatening remarks by Mr Blake that a refusal would mean that Mr Wray would never again be able to set foot behind the Iron Curtain. Still shocked by this sudden and unwelcome intrusion, Mr Wray, rather than expressing his instant refusal, told Mr. Blake that such a life-changing step required more thinking time and asked his visitor to leave.

Instead of using the internal telephone system, which was undoubtedly monitored, Mr Wray rushed to the chairman's room to inform him about the encounter with George Blake.

"We must get you out of Moscow as quickly as possible," the Chairman concluded, "and I will phone our Embassy right now to see if we can still speak to the Ambassador." And so a sequence of events quickly unfolded. The Embassy knew that the early British Airways flight was fully booked but one of the passengers was a member of the Embassy staff who would be told to delay his journey. "We shall send an Embassy car tomorrow morning to collect Mr Wray and take him to the check-in point at the airport where we have to ensure he is given the now vacant seat of our own staff member. Let us just hope," the Ambassador added, "that no problems arise at the passport control."

It was indeed Mr Wray's last visit behind the Iron Curtain. Having been his deputy manager I was now appointed as the acting Head of the East European Department. Mr Wray was given another senior role in the Millbank Office to deal with the different Trade Unions who were widely represented amongst ICI's large number of employees.

I am surprised that with your long and active involvement in the East European business you were only raised to acting Head of the Department.

In the immediate aftermath of the events in Moscow, I did not give this matter much thought, Joseph. The immediate substantial increase in my salary made me think that my nomination as Head of the Department was merely a question of time.

In any case, I was kept quite busy with the placement of our own candidates for the offices in Warsaw and Prague, necessitating further prompt visits to these countries.

It must have been just before the Christmas/New Year break when I became aware of rumours that a certain Mr French would become the new official Head of the East European Department starting in January. Naturally I was very disappointed. Was I seen as having become too vulnerable to potential pressures from East European intelligence agencies after so many years of contact with these countries? Had Mr Wray, in an attempt to protect me, leaked the episode with Oleg Lyalin which I had divulged to him prior to my attendance at the Moscow Trade Fair? I never found out.

Following a visit to the Yugoslav Embassy in London, I decided to make a brief exploratory trip to Belgrade. The initial discussion with the local authority was very positive and led, as I learnt later, to the establishment of a vibrant ICI Office with an English manager. My very last journey

East was on 6th of March 1977. Bucharest had suffered a ferocious earthquake two days earlier and our local manager, Rodescu, informed us via the UK Embassy that the building housing our office had suffered severe damage. On top of it we learnt that the other employee, Ana-Maria, had perished in her own home which had completely collapsed.

As the plane approached, Bucharest Airport a cloud of dust was still hanging over the city and on leaving the aircraft one was hit by a strange smell. The taxi driver confirmed that my favourite hotel, the Hilton, had survived the quake unharmed. His own home, he added, had fortunately only suffered a few minor cracks but the devastation in some parts of Bucharest had been horrendous. With bulldozers and groups of people doing their best to clear the roads we finally reached the hotel. As it was in walking distance from our office, I set off straight away to meet up with Rodescu. The street where the office was located was still littered with roof tiles and glass but at this end the buildings did not show any major structural damages. It was only when I progressed further down the street that the extent of damages became visible. The office building showed only a big crack above the main front door but once inside the building it was a scene of utter devastation. The whole upper floor had collapsed and the staircase was hanging upside down from the outer brick wall.

With such widespread destruction one had to assume that normal business relationships would have to be put on a temporary hold. I told Rodescu to stay at his own home, which being outside the city area had thankfully escaped the force of the quake. I added that on my return to the UK all ICI Divisions would be informed about the aftermath of this earthquake and would be asked to stop visiting Bucharest until he had established which Ministries and State Trading

Organisations had resumed working. Rodescu also wanted me to know that Ana-Maria had been a single girl without any family and that her local authority will most likely take care of her burial. He added that according to the first radio reports, an estimated 30,000 people had perished in this tragedy.

On my way back to the airport I once again paid a brief visit to the UK Embassy. It had not suffered any structural damages and the attaché informed me that a petition had already been sent to the Foreign and Commonwealth Office for some humanitarian help.

During the war years, I had witnessed the destruction of my home town Rostock and also the horrendous air raid on Hamburg in 1942 resulting in innumerable casualties but then, that was war. Now to see so much destruction in peace time left me decidedly shaken.

It was on my flight back to London that I began thinking more seriously about my future in the East European Department. Ever since I started working for ICI in 1963, a large part of my activity had been dealing with communist countries as far away as China. Maybe the time was ripe for a change. The newly appointed manager, who had no experience of business with state-controlled organisations and whose professional background seemed to have been more in the administrative sector, required regular and detailed briefings about the East European business. I began to find this quite tiresome.

It must have been early April when my previous manager, Mr Wray, paid me an unexpected visit in my office. Having always enjoyed a very friendly relationship with him, I took this opportunity to confide to him my concern about my own longer-term role in the Department. After listening to my lament, he said that he had heard on the company grapevine that ICI's Plant Protection Division, which, as I knew, was headquartered in a very pleasant rural location near my own home, was looking for a Business Development Manager for Western Europe. "I understand," he added, "that this will be quite a senior appointment. The normal flow of career progression is that people from ICI Divisions can move to the Company's London Head Office as happened in your own case but movements from here to Divisions are rare. Nevertheless, if you are interested, our central Personnel Department can easily make an official request for you to be interviewed." The thought alone of becoming involved in the world of agriculture was very appealing. It brought back memories again of my earlier years as an evacuee schoolboy when I became so enthralled by the life on that little farm in Mecklenburg that I could see myself involved in the world of agriculture in my own future adult life. And here we are. Fate seems to be on my side again.

Without any hesitation, I told Mr Wray that I would be interested. A week later I received an invitation to come for an interview at their headquarters in the village of Fernhurst. Whilst the different departments were housed in a number of wooden huts, reminding one of military barracks, I was directed to an old country mansion, the Verdley House where I was interviewed by one of the directors, Mr Johnstone and Mr Denise, the head of the West European Department. The job description sounded very exciting and I felt that the interview had gone well. A few days later I received a letter with a firm offer for the position, my remuneration and the starting date a month later to allow me to carry out a proper handover of my current functions in Millbank.

And so, Joseph, ended another chapter in my life, a life as you have now heard, full of ups and downs. Many of the earlier expectations of the NEW DAWN had come true and before the proverbial sunset, my retirement 16 years later, my professional and family life continued to be a source of exciting challenges, surprises and joyful moments which I may record one day.